Is English Changing?

Is English changing? To what degree is it changing? Is this change good or bad? In answering these questions, *Is English Changing?* provides a lively and concise introduction to language change, refuting commonly held misconceptions about language evolution as we understand it. Showing that English, like all living languages, has historically changed and continues to change, this book:

- analyzes developments in the lexicon, the way words are spoken or written, and the way in which speakers and writers use words;
- offers a basic overview of the major subfields of linguistics, including phonetics, morphology, syntax, semantics, pragmatics, and sociolinguistics, all viewed through the prism of language change;
- discusses change over time with examples from Old English, Middle English, and Modern English;
- reinforces important concepts with examples from other languages, including Spanish, Japanese, and Czech;
- clearly defines key terms and includes advice on rules, usage, and style, as well as ample annotated further reading and activities throughout.

Aimed at undergraduate students with little or no prior knowledge of linguistics, this book is essential reading for those studying this topic for the first time.

Steve Kleinedler is Executive Editor for the *American Heritage Dictionaries*.

Routledge Guides to Linguistics

Routledge Guides to Linguistics are a set of concise and accessible guidebooks that provide an overview of the fundamental principles of a subject area in a jargon-free and undaunting format. Designed for students of linguistics who are approaching a particular topic for the first time, or students who are considering studying linguistics and are eager to find out more about it, these books will both introduce the essentials of a subject and provide an ideal springboard for further study.

This series is published in conjunction with the Linguistic Society of America. Founded in 1924 to advance the scientific study of language, the LSA plays a critical role in supporting and disseminating linguistic scholarship both to professional linguists and to the general public.

Series Editor

Betty J. Birner is a Professor of Linguistics and Cognitive Science in the Department of English at Northern Illinois University.

Titles in this series:

Language in Children
Eve V. Clark

Ebonics
Sonja Lanehart

Why Study Linguistics?
Kristin Denham and Anne Lobeck

Language and Meaning
Betty J. Birner

Is English Changing?
Steve Kleinedler

Sign Languages
Diane Lillo-Martin, Sandra Wood and Joseph Hill

Bilingualism
Shahrzad Mahootian

More information about this series can be found at www.routledge.com/series/RGL

Linguistic Society of America

Is English Changing?

Steve Kleinedler

Routledge
Taylor & Francis Group

LONDON AND NEW YORK

First published 2018
by Routledge
2 Park Square, Milton Park, Abingdon, Oxon OX14 4RN

and by Routledge
711 Third Avenue, New York, NY 10017

Routledge is an imprint of the Taylor & Francis Group, an informa business

© 2018 Steve Kleinedler

British Library Cataloguing-in-Publication Data
A catalogue record for this book is available from the British Library

Library of Congress Cataloging-in-Publication Data
Names: Kleinedler, Steven Racek, author.
Title: Is English changing? / Steve Kleinedler.
Description: New York, NY : Routledge, 2018. | Series:
   Routledge guides to linguistics | Includes bibliographical
   references and index.
Identifiers: LCCN 2017050163| ISBN 9781138234673
   (hardcover : alk. paper) | ISBN 9781138234666
   (softcover : alk. paper) | ISBN 9781351114073 (ebook)
Subjects: LCSH: English language—Variation—History. |
   Linguistic change—History. | Languages in contact—
   History. | Linguistic change—Forecasting.
Classification: LCC PE1074.7 .K54 2018 | DDC 427—dc23
LC record available at https://lccn.loc.gov/2017050163

ISBN: 978-1-138-23467-3 (hbk)
ISBN: 978-1-138-23466-6 (pbk)
ISBN: 978-1-351-11407-3 (ebk)

Typeset in Times New Roman
by Apex CoVantage, LLC

Writing this book would have been impossible without the feedback, guidance, and support of many colleagues and friends. I must acknowledge Barbara Abbott, Michael Adams, Neil Bardhan, Peter Chipman, Anne Curzan, Janet DeCesaris, Alexander Francis, Elaine Francis, Scott Golder, Sarah Grey, Joan Houston Hall, Kirk Hazen, Katherine Connor Martin, Lisa McLendon, John McWhorter, Margaret Anne Miles, Lynne Murphy, Chuck Palmer, Joseph Pickett, Dennis R. Preston, Louise E. Robbins, Amy Roeder, Jerry Sadock, Cara Schmidt, Jesse Sheidlower, Kory Stamper, Malynne Sternstein, Patrick Taylor, Bert Vaux, Josef Vávra, Lise Winer, and Ben Zimmer, as well as my editor, decades-long collaborator, and friend Betty Birner. I must also thank Lizzie Cox at Taylor & Francis and Autumn Spaulding at ApexCovantage for their hard work and attention to detail that made the publication of this book possible. Of course, any mistakes and misrepresentations are entirely my own.

Contents

Figures

Acknowledgements

Grateful acknowledgement is made to the following for permission to reprint previously published material:

- **impact** usage note (Section 4.2.10): Copyright © 2018 by Houghton Mifflin Harcourt Publishing Company. Adapted and reproduced by permission from *The American Heritage Dictionary of the English Language, Fifth Edition.*
- **IPA vowel chart** (Section 2.2.1.1): www.internationalphonetic association.org/content/ipa-chart, available under a Creative Commons Attribution-Sharealike 3.0 Unported License. Copyright © 2015 International Phonetic Association.
- Portions of Section 6.3 are adapted from "Have Your Salt and Eat It, Too," by Steve Kleinedler and are reprinted by permission of *VERBATIM: The Language Quarterly.*

Chapter 1

Introduction

1.0 Is English changing?

Actually, it is easy to answer the question that the title of this book poses. Yes, the English language is changing.

You have a powerful tool for analyzing language: yourself. Take a few moments and reflect on your personal experience as a person who uses language. You should easily be able to pinpoint events from the last 15 years of your life that reflect change in the English language (and in any other language you might speak in addition to English).

Now, let's step back a little further in time.

- In the 1950s and 1960s, the Cold War escalated between the United States and the Soviet Union and their respective spheres of influence. Both countries wanted to be the first to land a spacecraft on the moon. This space race led to increased interest in astronomy and physics across all levels of education and in the popular culture.
- In the 1970s and 1980s, the processing power of computers expanded exponentially. Completely new occupations that involved computer technology developed, including programming and data analysis. The use of computers to streamline business operations began to affect the way people dealt with hospitals, banks, educational institutions, and government agencies.
- In the 1990s and the beginning of the 21st century, the development and proliferation of the internet rapidly intensified the degree to which people used computer technology in most aspects of their

lives. The way in which most people acquire news, get information, and maintain social connections changed drastically.

All of these developments had an effect on language. New words have entered the language. New senses of existing words have developed. There are new ways of communicating and exchanging information. Change is not a new phenomenon, however. Language change didn't begin after World War II.

A thousand years ago, written language was passed from generation to generation by scribes and monks. In the mid-1400s, the invention of the printing press made the written word much more widely available. In the 1800s, the development of the telegraph meant that messages could be sent across vast distances in short periods of time. Each development that has improved the ability to communicate a message has led to the growth and spread of language. With this growth and spread comes change.

Written forms of language only go back several thousand years. Egyptian hieroglyphs date back almost 48 centuries. The unrecorded history of language goes back much further. Some theories of language development propose that language arose in one location and spread across the earth, and other theories propose that language sprung up independently in multiple locations. Regardless of which theory represents what actually happened, the language you speak is different than that of your parents, and of their parents, and so on, running backward through a multitude of generations. Indeed, the language you yourself speak is different from what you spoke last year, or 10 years ago.

1.1 Welcome to the field of linguistics

The study of language is called LINGUISTICS. This textbook is a broad overview of the field of linguistics. It is written for people who have had little exposure to linguistic terminology. It does not assume familiarity with the subject matter. By using simple vocabulary and avoiding complicated terminology and philosophy, I hope that you will find abstract or difficult concepts easier to grasp. You will be asked to observe how you use language. These observations will help guide your understanding of basic linguistic concepts.

Each chapter explores a different subfield, such as sound, structure, meaning, context, and variation. You will be introduced to these subfields with a brief overview. Then, we'll look at features of that topic that show why *yes* is the answer to the question *Is language changing?*

Although *linguistics* refers to the study of language itself, this introductory textbook focuses primarily on linguistic phenomena in English. However, we will sometimes examine how some of the concepts being discussed manifest in other languages. If this survey of language and language change piques your interest, you are encouraged to pursue these topics at your educational institution or on your own.

Further study will provide you with the opportunity to learn how these components operate in a multitude of languages from many language families. If your school has a linguistics department, each of the topics we discuss is often the focus of an entire course, so if something interests you, look into it further! Regardless of the opportunities available to you at your school, you can also explore topics of interest in greater detail on your own. At the end of each chapter in this book, there will be a short list of books and online resources that expand upon some of the ideas addressed in the chapter.

The chief assertion of this chapter is that language is changing. The very act of expressing yourself keeps the language you're using current and vital. So, let's look at the flip side. What happens if there is no change? Languages that don't change are dead languages. They are frozen. New words are not added because there are no native speakers left to use them to communicate.

An unknown number of languages have been lost forever. If a population died out or was forced to learn a new language by a conquering people, the language used by that population is lost if there is no written record of it. (Documenting endangered languages is an important area of linguistic research. The Endangered Language Project at www.endangeredlanguages.com is an excellent resource.)

Scholars have reconstructed a handful of languages without a written record – primarily languages that modern languages have descended from. This reconstruction has been accomplished by examining the similarities and differences in those modern languages and their earlier forms. The prefix *proto–* describes a reconstructed language that language families descend from. One such reconstructed language is Proto-Indo-European, a distant ancestor of English.

Sometimes, scholars have become aware of dead languages of antiquity because of written artifacts that exist, such as Sumerian (one of the first written languages) or Etruscan (the language of the ancient country of Etruria in present-day Italy). Other languages, such as Ubykh, a language once spoken in the Caucasus (and later, after the population emigrated, Turkey), have only more recently become dead languages as the last living speakers themselves have died.[1]

Very rarely, a formerly dead language can be resuscitated. Perhaps the best-known example is Hebrew. Hebrew, as a spoken language, was displaced by Aramaic and other languages over time and eventually came to be used only in religious texts. In the late 1800s, Hebrew was revived as a spoken language when groups of Jews across the world began to learn it and use it instead of their native languages. More important to the process of reviving Hebrew, people who learned Hebrew as adults used it with their children. For these children, Hebrew was their native language. When the modern state of Israel was established in 1948, Hebrew was chosen as its national language. In the years since, millions of people have learned Hebrew as their first language.

Something you can do!

- List an example of a dead language from each continent.
- How many speakers did these languages have at their peak?
- What led to the extinction of these languages?

1.2 A brief comparison of Old English, Middle English, and Modern English

So far, we've only looked at a few broad, general statements regarding the fact that languages are changing, by virtue of their being used actively by speakers and writers for communication. A simple examination of historical English texts will easily demonstrate that the English language has changed considerably since Old English began to become distinct from other West Germanic languages around the sixth century CE. (Other West Germanic languages include German and Dutch; historically, the West Germanic language closest to English is Frisian, a language of the northern Netherlands.)

1.2.1 Old English

One of the earliest known works written in English is *Beowulf*, a poem written in Old English sometime between the 8th and 11th centuries. The name of its author is unknown. This poem tells the tale of a hero named Beowulf who defeats a monster named Grendel. Beowulf becomes king of an area that is now part of Sweden. Here are the first few lines of this poem:

Hwæt, we Gar-Dena	in gear-dagum
þeod-cyninga	þrym gefrunon,
hu ða æþelingas	ellen fremedon.

This is Old English, and it is almost entirely unrecognizable to speakers of Modern English. There are unfamiliar letters:

- the ASH, æ, pronounced like the 'a' in *bat*
- the THORN, þ, pronounced like the 'th' in *thin*
- the EDH, ð, pronounced like the 'th' in *the*

The only word in this passage that is the same in Modern English is *in*. (*Hu*, meaning "how," comes close.)

Beowulf has been translated in Modern English by many Old English scholars. The Irish poet Seamus Heaney published *Beowulf: A New Verse Translation* in 2012. In it, this passage reads as follows:

So. The Spear-Danes in days gone by
and the kings who ruled them had courage and greatness.
We have heard of those princes' heroic campaigns.

For comparison, here's how the first few lines of an earlier translation from 1910 reads. It is from the Harvard Classics series, translated by American educator Francis Gummere:

> O, praise of the prowess of people-kings
> of spear-armed Danes, in days long sped,
> we have heard, and what honor the athelings won!

The phrase *in gear-dagum*, for example, is translated in the Heaney version as "in days gone by" and in the Gummere version as "in days long sped."

Let's dig deeper and pick apart piece by piece the components of the Old English word *gear-dagum*. You'll start to see a few more similarities. In Old English, *g* before certain vowels, including *e*, is pronounced more like *y*. In fact, Old English *gear* means "year."

Something you can do!

An ETYMOLOGY shows the path a word has taken to get to its present form. Consult a dictionary that includes etymologies, so that you can see how the word *year* developed over the past centuries into its present Modern English form. Here are three dictionary entries for the word *year*:

- *American Heritage Dictionary*: ahdictionary.com/word/ search.html?q=year
- *Merriam-Webster's Collegiate Dictionary*: merriam-webster. com/dictionary/year
- *Oxford English Dictionary*: oed.com/view/Entry/231475 (If your institution doesn't subscribe to the online OED, access this entry at its associated free site at en.oxforddic tionaries.com/definition/year.)

The Modern English word *yore*, which means "time long past," also comes from Old English *gear*. Nowadays, the word is most commonly used in the phrase *days of yore*. Heaney translates the *gear* in *Beowulf* as "gone by."

The Old English word for "day" is *dæg*. Again, you can see a similarity to Modern English. If you're familiar with German, you'll see that the German word for "day" (*Tag*) shows a similarity as well. The Old English and Old German words for "day" come from the same source, and regular patterns in how sounds have changed over time explain why the Modern English and Modern German words are pronounced differently.

In Modern English, the way most singular nouns become plural is through the addition of *–s* on the end, such as *cat/cats*. We say that English shows inflection for NUMBER. Old English does too, and it also shows inflectional endings that indicate different relationships (called CASES) between the nouns and the words around them. (Inflections, along with the concepts of *number* and *case*, are covered in Chapter 3.) In Modern English, we see remnants of this case system with pronouns (*I/me/my*, *she/her/hers*) and with the possessive forms of nouns (*dog/dog's*).

One of the cases of Old English is called the dative case. The dative case is used to indicate that a noun is an indirect object. (The indirect object in the sentence *Olivia gave Mia the ball* is *Mia*.) The dative case is also used after certain prepositions, including *in*.

Dagum is the dative plural form of *dæg*. It is shown by the *–um* ending and the change of the vowel from *æ* to *a*. Therefore, *dagum* means "days" – specifically, it is the form of "days" that is used as an indirect object or after prepositions like *in*. *In gear-dagum* thus translates as "in yore-days" or, as Heaney says, "in days of old."

Reading ahead in *Beowulf*, you can see stronger relationships with Modern English. Line 11 reads *þæt wæs god cyning!* This is very similar to Heaney's translation "That was one good king!"

For the most part, though, you would need to study Old English (or use a version that has the original text on one side and the translation on the other) to make your way through *Beowulf* in the original Old English.

Something you can do!

- Find a copy of *Beowulf* online or at your library.
- Compare several lines with the Modern English translation.
- List other connections between Modern English and Old English that you find.

Two online resources for the Gummere translation are:

- poetryfoundation.org/poems-and-poets/poems/detail/ 50114
- literatureproject.com/beowulf/index.htm

1.2.2 Middle English

Moving forward to Middle English, we begin to see even more similarities with Modern English. In 1066, the Norman Conquest changed the English language considerably. The Norman language, spoken in Normandy, is a Romance language similar to French. When William the Conqueror became the king of England, the language of the Normans had a lasting effect on English. The Norman Conquest marked the beginning of the transition period between Old English and Middle English. The form of English used from roughly 1100 until the late 1400s is known as Middle English.

One of the best-known written examples of Middle English is *The Canterbury Tales*. This work was written in the late 1300s by the English poet Geoffrey Chaucer (c. 1343–1400). Here are the opening lines of *The Canterbury Tales*:

> Whan that Aprill with his shoures soote
> The droghte of march hath perced to the roote

Although this passage is well over 600 years old, you should be able to understand a great deal of it. In fact, with the knowledge that *shoures* means "showers" and *soote* means "sweet," you can probably fully comprehend the first two lines. Additionally, this rhyming couplet indicates that our word *sweet* once rhymed with *root*! From this snippet, we can see changes in vocabulary, pronunciation, and sentence structure.

You can find a copy of *The Canterbury Tales* online at librarius.com/cantales.htm. Many publishing companies have fine versions of Chaucer's work, such as the one edited by Jill Mann for Penguin Classics.

1.2.3 Modern English

Modern English is the form of English used since about 1500. The English playwright William Shakespeare (1564–1616) was one of the earliest writers in Modern English. Shakespeare is one of the best-known and most-read authors of his time. In the past 400 years, his works have been produced countless times. Dozens of phrases first written by him have become regular idioms, from "dead as a door-nail" to "set my teeth on edge." Here is a portion of *Romeo and Juliet*, Act II, scene 2, taken from the Second Folio:

> Whats Montague? it is nor hand nor foote,
> Nor arme nor face, o be some other name
> Belonging to a man.
> Whats in a name[?] that which we call a rose,
> By any other word would smell as sweete

It's easy to spot a few minor spelling differences (*foot/foote, arm/arme, sweet/sweete,* and *What's/Whats*). If you were expressing this thought nowadays, you might phrase it slightly differently, but it is nonetheless completely comprehensible.

You can access the full text of *Romeo and Juliet* at:

- shakespeare.mit.edu/romeo_juliet/full.html
- opensourceshakespeare.org/views/plays/playmenu.php?WorkID=romeojuliet

1.3 English is changing

To reiterate the theme of this textbook, language is changing. Individual shifts are part of a continuum of change. Even though the year 1100 is the cut-off between Old English and Middle English and 1500 is the cut-off between Middle English and Modern English, these points in time should not be thought of as representing an abrupt shift from one form of the language to another. Elements of Middle English in the beginning of its period are going to have more in common with elements of later Old English. Similarly, elements of later Middle English are going to have more in common with early Modern English.[2]

This quick look at evidence from Old English, Middle English, and the early days of Modern English should provide you with ample evidence that English has changed. And, if you browse newspaper archives from the beginning of the 1900s, even though you might find unusual turns of phrase, you should be able to understand almost everything you read. On an even shorter timescale, you should be able to quickly devise a list of words that were in vogue when you were in elementary school that have fallen out of your vocabulary. Likewise, there are words that were introduced then that are now an integral part of the language.

So, yes, it is clear that the English language has changed and continues to change. The language used in a Shakespeare play might sound old-fashioned. The dialogue in a 1940s film noir might sound quaint. The conversations in a coming-of-age teen comedy from the 1980s might sound ridiculous to modern ears. But all of these are representative of the English language.

Often when people ask whether language is changing, their questions stem from a fear of change. As far back as the Greek philosopher Socrates, older generations have bemoaned that the younger generations are talking incorrectly, or that the people from the other side of the tracks don't speak as well they do. When fear of what is new or different drives the discussion of change, change is often seen as something negative that affects the status quo.

In the 1960s, many people who wrote about language cringed at the thought of using *contact* as a verb (as in the sentence *Please contact me at your earliest convenience*). You've probably never heard of a rule that you shouldn't use *contact* as a verb, and it might seem odd or ridiculous that doing so was ever considered controversial. In the 1980s, as the pronunciation of *harass* shifted from HAIR-us to huh-RASS, there were many arguments regarding what pronunciation should be considered correct. Nowadays, the use of huh-RASS is completely unremarkable in the United States. In the current day, there's debate about whether use of *they* in the singular is acceptable, although such usage goes back several centuries. (All of these topics will be discussed later in the book.) There is a whole industry devoted to educating people on style and usage.

This would be an appropriate place to point out that I am a lexicographer – a person who compiles and edits dictionaries. Since 1997, I have been on the staff of the *American Heritage Dictionary of the English Language* and, since 2011, I have been its executive editor. As such, I frequently am contacted by traditionalists who bemoan what they consider to be the loose standards of spoken and written English, and by people who fear (or profit from making others fear) change and variation. If you're wondering how a dictionary editor could take a seemingly laid-back attitude toward language change, consider that, simply stated, the purpose of most dictionaries is to *describe* how language *is* used. Usage guidance is offered for those who are interested in the traditions of what are considered to be proper grammar, style, and usage. (Dictionaries and style guides are discussed in Chapter 8.)

Like most linguists, I believe that if you can communicate effectively, you are using language properly. There is a "rule" that states that you shouldn't split infinitives; that is, you shouldn't put words between *to* and the bare form of the verb, as in the oft-quoted example *to boldly go.* This "rule" is easily and often "broken," and people who split their infinitives are readily understood. The actual rules of English are ones that don't need to be taught to native speakers because native speakers learned them as infants and toddlers. Native speakers of English know without being taught that *the the mat cat on is* is not a well-formed sentence. The actual rules of English are those that allow you to identify sentences as *The cat is on the mat* or *It's the mat that the cat is on* as grammatical and strings like *the the mat mat cat on is* as ungrammatical.

Almost all linguists view change in language either neutrally or positively. A neutral viewpoint is one that change is change and is inherently neither good nor bad: it is merely change. A positive viewpoint is one that considers the effects of the change – the varieties of language that develop that distinguish the speaking patterns of different communities and locations across the globe – to be a positive force in keeping the language alive and dynamic.

Linguistic change itself is a neutral phenomenon to which no value judgment can be ascribed. It can be argued that the sociological changes that arise have either a neutral or a positive effect on the language itself and on its speakers and their culture. The philosophy that I reject in this book is the notion that language change and variation diminish the value of a language.

1.4 Overview of this book

In the following chapters, we will examine these areas of English:

- How English sounds (phonology)
- How English words are structured (morphology)
- How English sentences are structured (syntax)
- What English words mean (semantics)
- How context affects how English is understood (pragmatics)
- How English is influenced by social and cultural groups (sociolinguistics)
- How English varies from place to place (regional variation/ dialectology)

In addition to learning about the basic fundamentals of these topics, you will also see how the study of each area supports the statement that language is changing.

Lastly, in contrast to language rules that you implicitly learn as a native speaker, we will look at the arbitrary rules of English that are dictated, including spelling and usage. We will examine why these kinds of rules exist, and why efforts to prevent language from changing are usually futile.

This book is intended to give you an overview of the way English is structured, and how these structures undergo and have undergone change. It will emphasize how change is something that can be embraced rather than feared. Change will always be a part of a living language, and knowing about the linguistic phenomena that all languages share will allow you to take an interest in language as it is used around you.

Earlier in this chapter, you came across features called **Something you can do!** Throughout this book, this feature suggests a simple activity that challenges you to think about a topic in more detail. Sometimes questions are posed for you to think about; other activities involve discussion with other students.

If you want to delve deeper into the topics that are discussed, end-notes marked **Further Reading** point you toward publications that will help you explore that subject. (Full bibliographical information for these titles, along with all publications mentioned in the text, can be found in the References section beginning on page 173.)

Each chapter concludes with **Questions for Discussion**. These open-ended questions are intended to be a springboard for class discussion.

1.5 Questions for discussion

- Is language changing?
- What happens if a language stops changing?
- What is linguistics?
- How is Old English different from Modern English?
- How has English changed since you were born?
- If English is not your native language, how has your first language changed since you were born?

Notes

1 Further Reading: David Crystal, *Language Death*; Daniel Nettle and Suzanne Romaine, *The Extinction of the World's Languages*. Also, in "Salvaging the Dormant: On Language," Sarah Grey discusses linguists' efforts in working with indigenous communities who want to revitalize their languages or provide the tools for future generations to do so, refram-ing the metaphor of "dead" languages with "dormant" languages.
2 Further Reading: John Algeo and Carmen A. Butcher, *The Origins and Development of the English Language*; Laurel Brinton and Leslie Arnovick, *The English Language: A Linguistic History*.

Chapter 2

Speech sounds

2.0 Introduction

Wherever you happen to be reading or listening to these words, all around you are physical objects that you can see or touch. In the physical world, all matter is composed of one or more elements. If we were to analyze any object in the physical world by breaking it up into the smallest components that are distinct from one another, we would be examining individual atoms. A molecule of salt, for example, consists of one sodium atom and one chlorine atom.

If we analyze any spoken language by breaking up the stream of speech into components that are distinct from one another, we are left with dozens of individual sounds. Each of these individual sounds is called a PHONEME. Phonemes can be thought of in the same way as atoms. Sodium and chlorine atoms combine to form salt. Strings of phonemes combine to form sequences of sound. If these sequences are meaningful, they are manifestations of words, but they can also be gibberish.

In this chapter, we will examine:

- the process by which humans make sounds
- the way that linguists categorize these sounds
- the way that these sounds can combine in language
- how English pronunciation has changed over time
- how pronunciation of English varies across geographic regions
- processes by which sounds can change

The topic of PHONETICS involves the study of the inventory of sounds that humans produce by moving air through the vocal tract. The topic of PHONOLOGY involves the study of how these sounds are combined to form words or portions of words.

In the following description of the sounds of English, you'll see references to something called the INTERNATIONAL PHONETIC ALPHABET (or, for short, the IPA). The IPA was first developed in the late 1800s by the International Phonetic Association. (The abbreviation for the association is also IPA, but use of the abbreviation in this text refers to the alphabet. Their website, internationalphoneticassociation.org, is a very useful resource.) The International Phonetic Association has adjusted and expanded the IPA several times since its initial publication.[1]

The IPA consists of the inventory of sounds that humans can make in speech. When you see a symbol inside brackets – like [b] – those brackets are an indication that the character inside them refers to the symbol in the IPA and the sound that is represented by that symbol. For example, [b] is the phonetic symbol that corresponds to the first sound in the word *bed* or the final sound in *lob*. This bracketing convention contrasts [b], which represents the sound you make when speaking the word *bed*, with the unadorned use of *b* as a representation of the letter of the alphabet used when you write the words *bed* or *lob*.

2.1 The production of speech sounds

To create sound, air must flow through the vocal tract, typically from the lungs outward. You create some sounds, like the [b] in the word *bed*, when you vibrate your VOCAL FOLDS as air passes through them. (Vocal folds are also commonly known as VOCAL CORDS.) These folds are complex structures of muscle and mucosal tissue in your throat, and most people have two pairs of them. The upper pair is not involved in producing sound. When air expelled from the lungs passes through the lower pair of folds, the folds vibrate. For other sounds, like the [p] in the word *pat*, the vocal folds don't vibrate.

This stream of expelled air is modified by parts of your body in your mouth and near the inside of your mouth. (The inside of your mouth is also called the ORAL CAVITY.) The parts of the body that modify this air stream are called ARTICULATORS. These articulators include the:

- lips,
- teeth,
- tongue,
- HARD PALATE (the bony part of the roof of your mouth),
- SOFT PALATE (the soft part of the roof of your mouth past the bony part – this part is also called the VELUM), and
- PHARYNX (the part of your mouth past the soft palate but before the esophagus).

Something you can do!

- With the tip of your tongue, touch your lips, teeth, and hard palate.
- Raise the broad, flat part of your tongue or the back of your tongue to meet the soft palate.
- Pull the back of your tongue backward past the soft palate to meet the pharynx.
- What happens when you try to make sounds when your tongue is in each of these positions? We'll return to this exercise again at the end of the chapter.

One way that consonants are categorized is by the place in the mouth where they are articulated.

- Consonants that are articulated with the lips are called LABIALS. They include [p], [b], and [m].
- Consonants that are articulated with the tongue against the ridge of the roof of your mouth, just above your upper teeth, are called ALVEOLARS. They include [t], [d], and [n]. (This ridge is where the sockets of your teeth are located in the jaw. It is called the ALVEOLAR RIDGE.)
- Consonants that are articulated when the tongue and the velum meet are called VELARS. They include [k], [g], and [ŋ] (the sound represented by the letters 'ng' in words like *running*.) In English, [ŋ] never appears at the beginning of the word; however, in many other languages, it can.[2]

2.2 Kinds of speech sounds

Shortly after you learned the alphabet, you were likely taught that the letters of the alphabet were either consonants or vowels. Generally speaking, a VOWEL is created when you produce a steady, unobstructed flow of air. When you produce a CONSONANT, you're usually blocking or obstructing the flow of air in some manner.

2.2.1 Sonorants

More technically speaking, sound that is not obstructed is called a SONORANT. Sonorants include the vowels, but this category also includes some sounds that are classified as consonants.

2.2.1.1 Vowels

Something you can do!

Utter the following words aloud, slowly:

heat	hit
hate	het
hat	hot
hoed	hood
hoot	hut

Now do it a second time, paying attention to your tongue. Where is your tongue placed in your mouth when you make the sound of the vowel in each of these words?

When categorizing vowel sounds, we speak of positions, such as a high front vowel. These adjectives (*high, low, front, back, mid-*) refer to the position of your tongue in your oral cavity when you are making that vowel sound. So, for example, the vowel represented in the IPA as

[i] (which is the vowel in the word *heat*) is called a high front vowel. Say the word *heat* out loud, and feel where your tongue is when you make the vowel. This position contrasts with the vowel sound of the word *hoot*, whose vowel is represented by [u], which is a high back vowel. Alternate saying these two words and feel the position of your tongue in your mouth.

Imagine that you're looking at the inside of your mouth, from the side. The shape of the inside of your mouth is traditionally represented as an irregular trapezoid. Figure 2.1 shows you where the usual pronunciations of [i] and [u] are placed.

At this point, you might be wondering how [i] can represent the sound that in English you would associate with a long *e*. This is a good question. In part, English spelling conventions were formed a long time ago. Also, many of the original authors of the IPA were teachers of English from France, so that influenced their choice of letter symbols. And, English has undergone many sound changes over the centuries. (There will be examples of these changes later in the chapter.)

Consider a language like Spanish or Italian. In Spanish, the word *mi* means "my." In Italian, *mi* means "me." In both languages, *mi* is pronounced like the English word *me*. In Spanish and Italian, you can see a closer resemblance between the written symbol (*i*) and the sound that symbol represents in the IPA [i]. In English, you'll sometimes see this correspondence in many words of foreign origin that retain an *i*, as in *pita* and *patio*. Further, even though [i] is a single

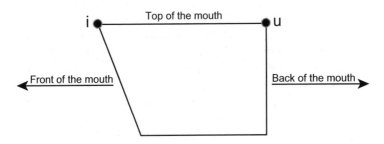

Figure 2.1 The placement of [i] and [u] on the IPA vowel chart.

vowel, it is often written in English with two characters, such as *ee* (as in *beet*) or *ea* (as in *heat*). (English has a lot of idiosyncratic spellings. There are other ways of representing this sound, too: *eo* of *people*, *ie* of *believe* and *relief*, *ei* of *deceive* and *conceit*, and *y* of *sanity* and *sticky*.)

Another important sound in English is a simple, unstressed, mid-central vowel called SCHWA. Its symbol is [ə], and it is conventionally used for unstressed vowels such as the *a* in *about*, the *i* in *pencil*, and the *u* in *hut*.

Generally speaking, in this chapter the word *vowel* is used to refer to vowel sounds and not the written characters (*a*, *e*, *i*, *o*, *u*) of the Roman alphabet used in languages like English.

There are a few ways vowels are categorized.

When you make back vowels, like [u] (like the *oo* in *hoot*) or [o] (a clipped version of the *o* in *rose*), your lips form a round shape. Such vowels are called ROUNDED. When you make front vowels, like [i] and [e] (a clipped version of the *a* in *hate*), you'll notice your lips are spread out. Such vowels are called UNROUNDED.

In English, front vowels tend to be unrounded and back vowels tend to be rounded. Other languages have rounded front vowels and unrounded back vowels. If you make an [i] with rounded lips, this sound is represented by the symbol [y]. In German, this sound is written *ü*. (When used to indicate a rounded vowel, the symbol ¨ is called an UMLAUT. In other contexts – for example, to indicate that two vowels are pronounced separately, as in *naïve* or *coöperate* – this symbol is called a DIERESIS.) If you make an [u] with unrounded lips, this sound is represented by the symbol [ɯ]. In Turkish, the letter that represents this sound is written as ı. (That's a lowercase *i* without the dot).

We also categorize vowels like [i] and [u] as HIGH, vowels like [o] and [e] as MID, and vowels like [æ] as LOW. (Pronounce *heat, hoot, hoed, hate*, and *hat* again and feel how your tongue is positioned.)

Vowels also show contrast in duration: they can be LONG or SHORT. [i] is a long vowel. Its short counterpart, [ɪ], is the sound of *i* in *hit*. (Say *heat* and *hit* aloud, and you will notice the difference.)

Additional symbols can be used to indicate a change in the manner of production. For example, the length of vowels is represented by a colon:

[e:] is an even longer version of the long vowel [e]. Nasalized vowels are represented with a tilde: [ẽ] is a nasal version of [e].

Figure 2.2 is a chart of the vowels used in the International Phonetic Alphabet. Some of these symbols represent sounds that are not part of the inventory of sounds of English.

The chief vowel sounds used in English are:

- [i]   heat, beet
- [ɪ]   hit, bit
- [ɛ]   het, bet
- [æ]   hat, bat
- [ɔ]   hot, cot (and, in some regions of the US, caught)
- [ʊ]   hood, good
- [u]   hoot, boot
- [ə], [ʌ] hut

VOWELS

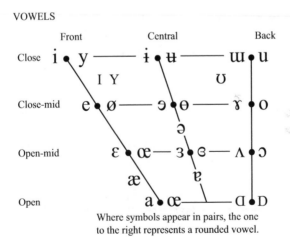

Where symbols appear in pairs, the one
to the right represents a rounded vowel.

Figure 2.2 The IPA vowel chart.

This chart is found by selecting "Vowel" from the list that is shown at www.internationalphoneticassociation.org/content/ipa-chart. It is available under a Creative Commons Attribution-Sharealike 3.0 Unported License.

(Some linguists use [ə] for unstressed syllables and [ʌ] in stressed syllables.)

You'll notice [e] and [o] are missing from this description. [e] is a clipped version of the *a* in *hate*. It is more like the *e* in the Spanish word *beso*. [o] is a clipped version of the *oe* in *hoed*. It is more like the *o* in the Spanish word *rosa*. That's because these sounds in English are diphthongs. A DIPHTHONG is two vowel sounds pronounced in sequence. There are three common diphthongs in English:

- [aɪ]   **i**ce, h**ei**ght, **eye**
- [eɪ]   h**a**te, **ei**ght, g**ai**t
- [oʊ]   t**o**ne, h**oe**d, t**oa**d, m**ow**ed

For example, the sound represented by the letter *i* in *ice* is actually a sequence of two sounds: [a] followed by [ɪ]. This sequence is represented as [aɪ] or [a̯ɪ].

These vowel sounds are VOICED. When you produce a voiced sound, your vocal cords vibrate as you push air past them. Sounds normally made without vibrating the vocal cords are called VOICELESS.

Something you can do!

This quick exercise should help you better understand the difference between voiced and voiceless sounds.

- Hold your throat with your hand.
- Alternate saying [s] and [z]. ([s] is the *s* in *sip*, [z] is the *z* in *zip*)
- Then lengthen the sounds: make a *sssssssss* sound, followed by a *zzzzzzzz* sound.

The vibration you feel when making the [z] sound is the result of voicing. [z] is voiced. [s] is voiceless.

When you don't vibrate the vocal cords for a sound that is normally voiced, that sound is DEVOICED.

The devoiced versions of these vowel sounds are usually represented in written English by the letter *h*. Try it: say *hate, hat, hot, heat*, and *hoop* again. The part of the word associated with the letter *h* in each of these words is actually a puff of air made without vibrating the vocal cords. This puff of air precedes the vowel sound while your lips are formed and your tongue is positioned in the location where you make the following vowel sound. This puff is simply represented by [h] in the IPA. (In a more precise version of the IPA, instead of using an [h], you use the same symbol as the vowel that follows, but with a hollow circle under it to indicate devoicing.)

2.2.1.2 Nasals, glides, and liquids

Some consonants are also considered to be sonorants: the nasals, glides, and liquids. (As you can see, the division of sounds into vowels and consonants is somewhat arbitrary. The nasals and the liquids are in many respects more like vowels than they are like consonants.)

NASALS are formed when the velum is lowered, which creates a nasal resonance when some of the airflow escapes through the nose. The nasals in English are all voiced. They are:

- [m]   **m**o**m**   labial nasal
- [n]   **n**u**n**   alveolar nasal
- [ŋ]   thi**ng**, runni**ng**   velar nasal

In English, [m] and [n] can appear at the beginning or end of a syllable, but [ŋ] appears only at the end of syllables. The symbol ŋ is called ENG or ENGMA.

LIQUIDS can be thought of consonants that can be prolonged like vowels. In some languages like Czech, liquids can serve as vowels, like in the words *vlk* "wolf" and *krk* "throat."

- [l]   **l**u**ll**
- [ɹ]   **r**oa**r**

Strictly transcribed, the 'r' of English is represented as [ɹ]. [r] is used to indicate a slight trill, as in Spanish *rosa*. However, when the IPA is being used to transcribe English and not in contrast to other languages, [r] is often used for convenience.

The IPA symbol [ɚ] is called SCHWAR (or RHOTIC SCHWA). It can be thought of as an *r*-like schwa or as a syllabic *r*. This sound is represented by the second syllable of *butter* in most varieties of English in the United States. In most varieties of English in England, this final syllable is nonrhotic and is merely a schwa sound. (*Rhotic* means "having to do with the pronunciation of *r*.")

Another important category are the GLIDES (which are also known as SEMIVOWELS). They are the transitional sounds that are made when moving from one sound to another. They include:

- [j]   beauty (a transition between the stop [b] and the vowel [u])
- [w]   towel (a transition between the diphthong [oʊ] and the liquid [l]

In some classification systems, glides and liquids are categorized together and called APPROXIMANTS.

2.2.2 Obstruents

An OBSTRUENT is a sound made when airflow is obstructed in some way. The consonants that aren't nasals, liquids, or glides are obstruents.

You can view sonorants and obstruents as two discrete categories. Or, you can view them on a continuum of sound production where one endpoint is completely unobstructed and the other is completely obstructed.

There are two main categories of obstruents: stops and fricatives. What differentiates these categories is whether the airflow is completely or partially obstructed during articulation.

2.2.2.1 Stops

One category of consonants found in almost all languages is STOPS. The stops are created when the outflow of the air is stopped. Although you can pronounce a vowel for as long as you'd like until you run out of breath, you can't lengthen a consonant. Compare [e] with [b]. You can force out a quick "buh" – and you can of course lengthen the "uh" part – but the [b] part is the sound made when, having brought your lips together, you open them while voicing sound.

[b] is voiced – that is, your vocal cords vibrate when you make this sound. The voiceless counterpart to [b] is [p]. (An exercise in the next section will help explain the difference!)

The stops in English are:

- [p]   **pop**   voiceless labial stop
- [t]   **tot**   voiceless alveolar stop
- [k]   **kick**   voiceless velar stop
- [b]   **bob**   voiced labial stop
- [d]   **did**   voiced alveolar stop
- [g]   **gag**   voiced velar stop

Something you can do!

- Alternate saying *buh* and *puh* several times.
- Alternate saying *tuh* and *duh* several times.
- Alternate saying *kuh* and *guh* several times.
- Describe the differences (and the similarities) for each pair.

Other languages have additional stops. For example, past the soft palate is the UVULA. (It's that little fleshy projection that hangs down from the back of the roof of your mouth.) You can make uvular stops by touching the uvula with the back of the tongue. The voiceless uvular stop is represented by [q]. It is used in Arabic and many languages of Central Asia, for example. The unvoiced uvular stop is represented by [ɢ], but it is less common than [q].

2.2.2.2 Fricatives

FRICATIVES are formed when the airflow is forced through the mouth in a way that narrows the passage:

LABIODENTALS are formed by placing the lower lip behind the upper teeth.

- [f]   **fat**   voiceless
- [v]   **vat**   voiced

INTERDENTALS are formed by placing the tongue between the teeth. Although there are two different sounds, they are usually both represented in written English by the letters *th*:

- [θ]   **the**   voiceless
- [ð]   **th**in   voiced

SIBILANTS are formed by directing a jet of air at an obstruction and using the tongue to channel airflow toward the upper teeth or alveolar ridge.

- [s]   **s**ip   voiceless
- [z]   **z**ip   voiced
- [ʃ]   **sh**ip   voiceless
- [ʒ]   mea**s**ure   voiced

AFFRICATES are a combination: a stop followed by a fricative.

- [ts]   wal**tz**   voiceless
- [tʃ]   **ch**at   voiced

[ts] occurs at the beginning of words in other languages like German, as in *Zeit* ("time"), pronounced [tsaɪt]. *Tsar*, a word that English has borrowed from Russian, begins with this sound, too.

A common fricative that doesn't occur in English is the voiceless uvular fricative [x]. This is the final consonant sound of the Scots Gaelic word *loch* (meaning "lake") or the German name *Bach*. The voiced counterpart [ʁ] is a prominent feature of French phonology. In French, words beginning with the letter *r* are pronounced this way.

2.2.3 Consonant clusters

A CONSONANT CLUSTER is a sequence of two or more consonants. In English, [kl] (as in *clean*), [str] (as in *string*), and [rd] (as in *third*) are examples of consonant clusters. Some clusters only occur in certain positions in syllables; for example, [rd] in English appears only at the ends of syllables. Some consonant clusters occur in some languages, but not others: [tsv] is an example of a cluster that occurs in Czech but not English. [gb] is a cluster that occurs in many West African languages, such as the Gbe language family, but not in European languages. Other languages, like Hawaiian and Chinese, do not permit consonant clusters.

The combination of sounds that are allowed and not allowed in a language is known as the PHONOTACTICS of that language.

You can produce a string of sounds that does not form a word in particular language. In English, *glorpee, vzcvrnkls*, and *lrgbfmg* are strings of sounds, but they are not words. You can probably pronounce *glorpee*, but it has no meaning in English. On the model of words like *payee* or *mentee*, you might imagine it could mean "a person who is glorped." *Vzcvrnkls* has no meaning in English, and most English speakers might have a difficult time trying to pronounce it. However, it is a word in Czech: it is the second-person singular past tense of a verb used to describe the action of flipping an object resting on your thumb against your first finger upward. (If you're familiar with tiddlywinks, this is the motion used to flip one.) *Lvgbfmg* is largely unpronounceable and has no meaning.

Glorpee adheres to the phonotactic inventory of English. *Vzcvrnkls* (*c* is pronounced [ts] in Czech) is allowed in the phonotactics of Czech, but not of English. *Lvgbfmg* violates the phonotactics of not only English but probably almost every other language as well.

2.2.4 Other means of sound production

So far, we've discussed the production of speech sounds in terms of airflow that is unimpeded or obstructed. There are other ways to make sounds with your vocal tract. CLICKS are one example. One kind of click is the sound represented in written English by the phrase *tsk tsk tsk*, made by clicking the tongue against the roof of the mouth. Clicks are generally found in the languages of the Khoisan family of south-western Africa and the Nguni languages (including Xhosa and Zulu) of the Bantu family in southern Africa.

2.3 Syllable structure

Words are composed of syllables. A SYLLABLE is a unit of sound that consists of a central sound, usually a vowel or a diphthong, and option-ally a consonant or consonant cluster on either or both sides of that vowel or diphthong.

Many words have only one syllable: *bench, light, port*. Examples of words with two syllables are *apple, moonlight*, and *singing*.

Syllables are composed of three parts. Two of these parts are optional.

The center of the syllable is the NUCLEUS. The nucleus is generally a vowel or diphthong, but it can also be a liquid or nasal.

If a syllable begins with a consonant or consonant cluster, that part is known as the HEAD. If a syllable ends with a consonant or consonant cluster, that part is known as the CODA. In English, a syllable must have a nucleus, and the head and coda are optional.

head	nucleus	coda	
[s]	[i]	[t]	[sit] = seat
[ʃ]	[aɪ]	[n]	[ʃaɪn] = shine
[str]	[i]	[t]	[strit] = street

As mentioned at the beginning of this chapter, phonology describes how these sounds are combined to form words or portions of words.

An important part of phonology is understanding the phoneme. Up until this point, we've been talking about sounds: the isolated symbol [p], for example, represents the same sound across languages. How-ever, what might appear to be the same sound actually differs depend-ing on the environment. Sometimes this difference is hard to notice because in the written system the same letter is used to represent the different ways the sound is used.

[p] provides a good example. At first glance, you might think the 'p' sounds in *spit* and *pit* are identical. But they're not!

Something you can do!

- Place your hand in front of your mouth.
- Say *spit* and *pit* aloud.
- Describe any differences you notice.

When you say *pit*, there's a puff of air that comes out when you pronounce the 'p'. This puff of air is called ASPIRATION. You don't make this puff of air when you say *spit*. In the IPA, aspiration is indicated with a superscript [ʰ]. (A superscript character is written above and to the side of another character, often in a smaller size.)

spit   [spɪt]
pit   [pʰit]

In English, when a voiceless consonant (like [s]) is followed by a voiced stop (like [p]), the voiced sound becomes devoiced. This is an example of ASSIMILATION. When a sound undergoes assimilation, it takes on a feature associated with another sound near it. In this case, the [s] is voiceless. The [p], which is normally aspirated, becomes DEASPIRATED. Both sounds are made without vibrating the vocal cords. The [p] of *spit* is a devoiced [b]. If you're using a refined version of the IPA with special marks, the [p] would be written as [b] with a small hollow circle under the b.

In English, [p] and [pʰ] are called ALLOPHONES of the phoneme /p/.

By convention, phonetic symbols are enclosed in brackets, like [p]. Phonemes are enclosed in slashes, like /p/. Allophones do not show contrast in a language. For example: in English, [b] and [p] are CONTRASTIVE (that is, they show contrast). *Bit* and *pit* are different words. In English, [p] and [pʰ] are *not* contrastive. In some languages, [p] and [pʰ] *are* contrastive. Thai is an example. In Thai, [pɪt] and [pʰɪt] are the pronunciations of two different words.

So, the phonological rules of English include:

* When a voiced consonant follows a voiceless consonant, it becomes devoiced.
* Voiceless stops are aspirated unless preceded by a voiced consonant.

If English is your native language, you were never taught these rules. Likely you were unaware of them until now. You naturally picked up these rules as you learned how to speak. Throughout this book I'll be pointing out the difference between rules you know as a native speaker and rules you are taught as a convention of the language.

2.4 Kinds of sound changes

The development of languages over time shows similar characteristics. The following section describes kinds of sound changes along with examples of these changes, mostly from English. Broadly speaking, we will be looking at four kinds of changes: changes involving the loss of sounds, changes involving the addition of sounds, changes involving the transposition of sounds, and changes due to the influence of nearby sounds.

2.4.1 Loss of sounds

APHERESIS occurs when you drop one or more sounds or syllables from the beginning of a word. *Possum* from *opossum*, *coon* from *raccoon*, *tater* for *potato*, and *tween* for *between* are all examples. Other examples are drops in phrases, like *'twas* for *it was* and *'tis* for *it is*. You'll find poets and other writers of verse such as Shakespeare employing apheresis (and many of the other kinds of changes in this section) to maintain the meter of a piece. Many words that begin with 'kn,' like *knife* and *knight*, were pronounced in Middle English with the [k] sound preceding the [n] sound. The [k] dropped out via apheresis; however, the spelling was retained.

SYNCOPE occurs when you drop one or more sounds or syllables from the middle of a word. Consider the British English pronunciation of *secretary* as though it were spelled *secret'ry*. Some words might have multiple drops, as is the case with many navigation terms, like *forecastle*, which is pronounced *foksul* and is indeed often spelled *fo'c'sle*. Syncope is common in verse, such as *o'er* for *over*.

APOCOPE occurs when you drop one or more sounds from the end of a word. Examples include *ad* for *advertisement*, *litho* for *lithograph*, *psych* for *psychology*. These words are also known as CLIPPINGS, and this is an extremely productive process in English. Many common words were shortened in this way, for example: *taxi cab* is a shortened form of *taximeter cabriolet*. In verse, you'll see *ope* used for *open*, for example.

Something you can do!

- Create a list of words that have undergone apheresis, syncope, or apocope. Try to list five words for each category.
- Which of these words do you consider to be slang, and which do you think are now standard words in English?

HAPLOLOGY occurs when a syllable that occurs next to the same or a similar syllable is dropped. In English, possession is indicated by adding –'s. If a word already ends with the [s] sound, the possessive form of these words is not pronounced.

For example: The possessive form of *cat* is *cat's*. The plural of *cat* is *cats*, and the plural form of the possessive is *cats'*. The possessive form of the singular is made by adding the [s] sound. The plural form is also made by adding the [s] sound. But the possessive plural form *cats'* is still just [kæts], not [kætsɪz]. This is also true when forming the possessive of some names that end with an [s] sound, like that of the dramatist Euripides.

2.4.2 Addition of sounds

EPENTHESIS occurs when you insert one or more sounds into a word, especially in the middle of a word. The pronunciation of *athlete* with three syllables (ath-uh-lete) or *film* with two syllables (fill-um) are examples.

Often the inserted sound is a schwa, in order to make unusual consonant clusters easier to pronounce. However, the added sound isn't always a schwa. For example, the Modern English word *thunder* was *þunor* in Old English. *Hamster* is often pronounced with an epenthetic *p*, as though it were spelled *hampster.* When languages borrow words from other languages that have less restrictive rules on consonant clusters, epenthetic vowels are often introduced, such as the [u] and the second [o] in *okesutora*, the Japanese word for *orchestra.* When epenthesis occurs at the beginning of the word, it is also known as PROSTHESIS. Many Latin words that begin with [s] begin in Spanish with [ɛs]: the word *foam* is *spuma* in Latin and *espuma* in Spanish. Although this is a less common phonological process in English, *shyeah* for *yeah* is an example.

REDUPLICATION occurs when you repeat a sound or syllable. In English, reduplication frequently manifests itself in baby talk: *night night, peepee.* Words like *namby-pamby, pell-mell*, and *willy-nilly* are said to exhibit rhyming reduplication. In other languages, reduplication can indicate a change in the function of a word.

2.4.3 Transposition of sounds

METATHESIS occurs when two sounds are transposed within a word. In Old English, *bird* was spelled *brid*. The middle sounds transposed during the Middle English period. The pronunciation of *ask* as though it were spelled *aks* or *ax* is another example, discussed at greater length in Section 8.2.1.

Examples of metathesis across word boundaries are usually called SPOONERISMS, such as *mice to neat you* for *nice to meet you* or *sand hanitizer* for *hand sanitizer*. Spoonerisms are named for William Archibald Spooner, a British cleric who was known for making these kinds of errors in speech.

2.4.4 Change from influence of nearby sounds

DISSIMILATION occurs when you change a sound when it is similar to a nearby sound to something else. The most well-known examples in English are the dropping of the first *r* in *February* and *library*.

As noted earlier, ASSIMILATION occurs when you change a sound to be like a nearby sound. Usually it takes place in a word where, instead of using two distinct places of articulation in succession, you use just one. In compound words where one syllable ends with an alveolar consonant and is followed by a labial consonant, often the alveolar consonant will become labialized. *Sandbox*, especially in rapid speech, would be pronounced [sæmbɔks], where the alveolar cluster [nd] has assimilated to the labial [m] before [b].

2.5 Changes in sound over time

Now that you've got the basic underpinnings of the sound inventory of English, we can look at ways that language changes phonologically over time. Not only do words change their meaning, but the way sounds are pronounced changes over time.

Scholars long knew that Greek and Latin shared similarities and found that they ultimately came from a similar source. In the 19th century, linguists studying Sanskrit saw patterns that indicated that it, too, shared similarities. And by looking at similarities between languages, linguists could reconstruct what this earlier language, which came to be known as Proto-Indo-European (abbreviated PIE), looked like.

By studying regular sound changes over time, linguists are able to categorize how many of the languages from Europe to India are related. Proto-Indo-European developed around 5000 BCE, somewhere between what is now Eastern Europe and the Aral Sea. Some of the language families that descended from PIE have died out. For example, the Tocharian family consists of Tocharian A and Tocharian B. The only evidence for their existence comes from artifacts that have been excavated in northwestern China, including religious texts and permits associated with local caravan routes.[3]

There are eight branches of the Indo-European family of languages that descended from PIE whose descendants include living languages:

- **Germanic** – The North Germanic languages include Swedish and Danish. The West Germanic languages include German, Dutch,

English, and the closest relative to English, Frisian. There's one East Germanic language, Gothic, and it died around the sixth century CE.

- **Balto-Slavic** – The Baltic languages consists of Lithuanian and Latvian. The Slavic languages are divided among three groups: West Slavic (including Polish, Czech, and Slovak), South Slavic (including Slovene, Serbian, Croatian, and Bulgarian), and East Slavic (including Russian and Ukrainian).
- **Celtic** – Celtic languages include Irish Gaelic, Scots Gaelic, and Welsh, all of which are currently undergoing revitalization.
- **Italic** – Italic languages include those descended from Latin (collectively known as the ROMANCE languages, which include Portuguese, Spanish, Catalan, French, Italian, and Romanian) and several dead languages that were spoken on the Italian peninsula, including Umbrian.
- **Albanian**
- **Armenian**
- **Hellenic** (Greek)
- **Indo-Iranian** – The Indic languages include Sanskrit, Bengali, Sinhalese, Gujarati, Hindi, Urdu, and Romany. The Iranian languages include Pashto, Kurdish, Tajik, and Farsi.

One example of regular changes in sounds among Indo-European languages is known as GRIMM'S LAW, named for its discoverer, Jacob Grimm. (You might also know him as one of the brothers who wrote Grimm's fairy tales – he was not just a writer but a linguist, too.) Grimm's Law shows a relationship between consonants in PIE and the Germanic languages. For example, the sounds [b], [d], and [g] in PIE became [p], [t], and [k] in Germanic languages. The English word *cold* (and its German cognate *kalt*) comes from an PIE root, *gel-*. (Because Latin didn't undergo this change, many English words that derive from Latin and have to do with coldness, such as *glacier* or *gelid*, are pronounced with [g] or the "soft *g*" [dʒ] rather than with [k].) This b d g → p t k shift is just one of several shifts that Grimm's Law describes. A comprehensive dictionary will show etymological information such as this.[4]

Sometimes the pronunciation of a word shifts in a relatively short period of time. Since its inception in the 1960s, the *American Heritage Dictionary (AHD)* has enhanced many of its entries with usage notes based on the feedback of its usage panel. This panel has consisted of 130 to 180 people who are known for their writing abilities: novelists, columnists, essayists, playwrights, linguists, even crossword-puzzle makers. Each year, the *AHD* editorial staff polls the panelists about a few dozen topics. One item that's been balloted over the years is the panelists' preferred pronunciation of *harass*.

Before 2000, the pronunciation of *harass* was an oft-cited example of a word where two different pronunciations existed in opposition to each other: roughly, HARE-uhs, with stress on the first syllable, and huh-RASS, with stress on the second syllable. As recently as 1987, preference among the *AHD* panelists was split almost 50/50. When dictionary editors (including me) conducted interviews, one common question was about the "proper" pronunciation of *harass*. By 2001, the preference of the panel had shifted to 70/30 in favor of huh-RASS, and by 2013 to 90/10. (What's more, in 2013, more than a third of the panel found the original, traditional pronunciation, HARE-uhs, to be unacceptable). In 25 years, its pronunciation shifted from a toss-up to a clear preference. The change in acceptance of the newer form came about remarkably fast, at least in the United States. (The pronunciation with initial stress is still favored in the United Kingdom.)

2.6 Changes in sound from place to place

Sound changes are also responsible for different pronunciations in different dialects. If you are used to using dictionaries published in the United States and haven't studied foreign languages, the IPA system is probably new to you. Because vowels are pronounced differently across the United States, most American dictionaries will use a pronunciation guide that connects sounds to a key. For example, the symbol ŏ might be keyed to the word *pot*. But the way *pot* is said in Chicago is different than the way *pot* is said in Boston. The vowel in *might* is pronounced differently in the northern United States than in the South. Because there is no one "correct" system of American

English, pronunciation guides that are connected to a key will orient the user to their own way of speaking.

There is no one regional accent in the United States whose features represent what could be called a standard American accent. People allude to various newscasters speaking "without an accent," and although you can work to remove traces of specific accents in your speech, there is no one region that lacks all regional markers.

Sometimes the sounds of a particular area will change over time. One well-known example is the Northern Cities Shift (also called the Northern Cities Vowel Shift). At some point several decades ago, certain speakers in a region roughly running from Troy, New York, to the middle of Wisconsin and roughly north of Interstate 90 began pronouncing some vowels higher and further back, which caused other vowels to also change position in the mouth. As with many language shifts, the originators of the shift tended to be younger women. This shift started in population centers and gradually spread into rural areas, usually following the paths of interstate highways.

You can hear examples of the Northern Cities Shift in movies and shows set in Chicago and other areas in the upper Midwest. People sometimes refer to these Midwest vowels as broad or flat. Studies have shown how this pattern has spread since the 1960s. *American Speech*, the journal of the American Dialect Society, has published dozens of articles over the years about the phenomenon of vowel shifts, and it is a good resource to learn more about these patterns. (If your school has access to Project MUSE, you can read articles from *American Speech* online.[5])

An example of sound shifts in the United Kingdom is the phenomenon known as *th*-FRONTING. This is the process by which 'th' becomes pronounced as [f] or [v]. The voiceless [θ] becomes [f] – *think* is pronounced as though it were spelled "fink." The voiced [ð] becomes [v] – *bother* is pronounced as though it were spelled "bovver." The voiceless shift occurs in any environment; the voiced shift does not occur at the beginnings of words (one doesn't say "vat" for *that*). This shift is part of the Cockney dialect and other dialects centered on London. In recent decades, though, this fronting has spread beyond London.

We discussed dead languages in Chapter 1. Dialects of a language can die out, too, often over the course of several generations. This process is called DIALECT LEVELING. For any of a number of sociological reasons, members of a speech community might change the way they speak over time. There might be an economic benefit to using the dialect of a different socioeconomic class. Sometimes the change is caused by contact between two dialects stemming from the migration of a population. In other cases, a population is forced to adopt the variety that has been declared to be official.[6]

In some communities, speakers continue to use different dialects in different settings. Such speakers are said to be BIDIALECTAL. In other communities, whether by choice or imposition, the less economically favored variety falls out of use and, over time, a dialect is lost.

Pronunciation differences among the various varieties of English across the globe are well-documented and well-known. Speakers of English in the United States and United Kingdom pronounce a wide array of ordinary words, from *garage* to *laboratory*, differently. But even within a speech community, variation exists and can change over time. Within the United States, even within the same dialect regions, there may be disagreements on how to pronounce *cumin, almond, pecan*, and *often*, to name a few.

Technological advances make it easier to study the properties of sound. Obtaining information in the form of spoken samples is much easier. A hundred years ago, researchers needed to transcribe the spoken word (usually using the IPA to painstakingly write down what people said) to create maps of dialect boundaries. Decades later, research entailed carrying around heavy recording equipment and then transcribing the recordings. Each technological advance makes it quicker and easier to record interviews. Nowadays, the processing power of even the simplest computers allows for precise mathematical calculations to determine the frequencies of uttered sound, which once had to be calculated by hand.

The internet allows researchers to poll millions of people in a short period of time. Researchers for the *Dictionary of American Regional English* in the 1960s visited hundreds of towns across the country to conduct interviews. These interviews yielded hundreds of maps and a six-volume dictionary that compiled varieties of speech across the country. Similar dialect atlases were made in Great Britain and elsewhere.

One aspect of these dictionaries and dialect atlases is dialect maps that show where different regions of the country use different pronunciations. Much like the line on a weather map that shows the boundary between temperatures in the 20s and temperatures in the 30s, these maps have lines (called ISOGLOSSES) that mark off change boundaries. For example, in some parts of the United States, people pronounce the 's' of *greasy* with an [s]; in other parts of the country it's pronounced with a [z]. The boundary that separates those two areas is an isogloss.

These dialect maps were once compiled by plotting data points on a map. Now, by asking people to respond to quizzes on the internet, thousands or millions of points of data can be used to create a HEAT MAP – a multicolored map that shows differences (as in in phonology or vocabulary) with a great degree of gradation.

Something you can do!

* Visit projects.alc.manchester.ac.uk/ukdialectmaps. This is the website for "Our Dialects," a project run by the University of Manchester in the United Kingdom.
* Compare the following maps. The first shows regions where the words *pour* and *poor* are pronounced the same. The second shows where the words *class* and *farce* don't rhyme.
projects.alc.manchester.ac.uk/ukdialectmaps/phonological-variation/pour-poor
projects.alc.manchester.ac.uk/ukdialectmaps/phonological-variation/class-farce

---

We'll continue exploring dialect atlases in section 7.4.

2.7 Conclusion

In this chapter, we've looked at the individual sounds that make up the speech sounds of English. We've looked at the ways these sounds combine, how variation in these sounds has occurred over time, and how variation in these sounds exists now, over distance. In the next chapter, we'll be looking at meaningful components of words.

2.8 Questions for discussion

- What are the parts of the oral cavity?
- How are vowels and consonants different?
- How are vowels and consonants alike?
- How are sonorants and obstruents different?
- Repeat the **Something you can do!** exercise from section 2.1. How is your response the same or different from when you did it the first time?
- What are some ways that sounds change over time?
- Make a list of words that are pronounced differently in different parts of your country and discuss any patterns that you notice.

Notes

1 Further Reading: Arika Okrent, "11 Fun Facts about the International Phonetic Alphabet" (online access at http://mentalfloss.com/article/83340/11-fun-facts-about-international-phonetic-alphabet).
2 Further Reading: Many IPA symbols, like [ŋ], aren't part of the Roman alphabet. Descriptions of all IPA symbols can be found in *Phonetic Style Guide*, by Geoffrey K. Pullum and William A. Ladusaw.
3 Further Reading: The Museum Tusculanum Press in Copenhagen, Denmark, publishes an academic journal called *Tocharian and Indo-European Studies*.
4 Further Reading: Calvert Watkins (editor), *American Heritage Dictionary of Indo-European Roots*; Robert McColl Millar (editor), *Trask's Historical Linguistics*, especially chapter 4.
5 Further Reading: Rob Mifsud, "How Americans near the Great Lakes Are Radically Changing the Sound of English" (online access at www.slate.com/articles/life/the_good_word/2012/08/northern_cities_vowel_shift_how_americans_in_the_great_lakes_region_are_revolutionizing_english_.html).
6 Further Reading: Ann Williams and Paul Kerswill, "Dialect Levelling: Change and Continuity in Milton Keynes, Reading and Hull."

Chapter 3

Word structure

3.0 Introduction

In the last chapter, we discussed phonetics, the study of the individual units of sound that people produce with their vocal tracts. We also discussed phonology, the study of how people combine these sounds to form syllables and words.

In this chapter, we will take a closer look at the structure of words. We will examine the individual parts that make up words – chunks of sound that have meaning. Some of these chunks are themselves words. Other chunks are not words in isolation, but combine with other chunks to form words. Specifically, we will examine:

- how words can be made up of smaller, meaningful chunks
- how linguists categorize these chunks
- how these chunks can combine in language
- how the structure of words has changed over time

3.1 Morphemes

Just like a series of phonetic sounds can be strung together to form a syllable, a word can consist of a string of word-parts. The study of these parts that make up words is called MORPHOLOGY. The translation of the Greek word *morphē* is "form" or "shape." This term is also found in other sciences to refer to form – in biology, for example, morphology deals with the form and structures of organisms.

I've been using the terms *chunk* and *word-part* to describe this basic structural feature. MORPHEME is the technical name. This naming convention is intentionally analogous to the vocabulary used to describe sound. A phoneme is a basic unit in phonology. When French linguists were developing morphological theory, they chose the *–eme* ending to refer to this structural unit.

A morpheme cannot be divided into smaller units of meaning. Some words are themselves morphemes:

* Nouns like *cat, house, justice, town*
* Verbs like *go, bake, run, swim*
* Adjectives like *red, glad, wet, large*

Sometimes these simple forms are called the BASE or ROOT form. Other morphemes can be added to these forms.

3.1.1 Affixes

Some morphemes can't stand alone as words themselves. You're familiar with prefixes and suffixes in English. These are good examples of morphemes that have meaning but are not themselves words.

Prefixes, suffixes, and infixes are known as AFFIXES.

A PREFIX is a morpheme that is added to the beginning of a word. One example is *un–*. Actually, *two* prefixes are spelled this way:

* The first prefix spelled *un–* is usually placed in front of an adjective. It means "not." Someone who is *unwell* is *not well*. Sometimes this prefix can be used in front of nouns, too, as in *unconcern*.
* The second prefix spelled *un–* is used in front verbs to express reversal or removal, as in *untie* or *unwrap.*

These two prefixes are spelled the same, in part because the historical development of the prefix used with verbs was influenced by the one used with adjectives. However, they originally come from different source words if you trace their history back to Proto-Indo-European. (Nouns, verbs, adjectives, and other parts of speech are defined in section 4.2 if you need a refresher.)

A SUFFIX is a morpheme that is added to the end of a word. One example is –*s*. Two different suffixes are spelled this way. One suffix is attached to verbs that appear with third-person singular nouns, pronouns, and noun phrases to indicate the present tense – meaning that the action is happening now. (This is in contrast to past-tense forms (like *ran* and *knew*) that indicate that the action happened in the past.)

he runs   she knows
it smells   Darryl laughs
Lilah sings   my sister waves
the man with the red hat dances

The second suffix that is spelled –*s* is used with many nouns to show the plural form.

table   tables
car   cars
toe   toes

Although you're most familiar with suffixes and affixes, there is another third kind of morpheme that attaches to a word. An INFIX is placed in the middle of a word.

As you saw above, the suffix –*s* is added to verbs to form the third-person singular present tense. Scholars have determined that in Proto-Indo-European, one of the many ways to form the present tense of a word was by using the infix –*n*– or –*ne*– . This infix survives in English in the word *stand*. Compare this present tense form with its past tense form *stood*. The –*n*– in *stand* is a remnant of this very old infix that indicated present tense.

Although infixes are an important structural component of some languages, English doesn't employ infixation to produce more words very often. Infixing is used most often in English to create slang words, usually with infixes that make the resulting word more emphatic (and more vulgar). One of the most common examples in English is *fucking*, as in *absofuckinglutely* and *infuck-ingcredible*. Similarly sounding (and less vulgar) words like *frick-ing* or *flipping* can achieve the same effect.

Most affixes are INFLECTIONAL or DERIVATIONAL. Whether an affix is inflectional or derivational depends on its function.

3.1.1.1 Inflectional affixes

An inflectional affix changes the grammatical function of a word. Prefixes, infixes, or suffixes can be inflectional, but in English, inflectional affixes are usually suffixes.

A form of a word that is made by adding an inflectional suffix to the root is called an INFLECTION or an INFLECTED FORM.

* *Apples* is an inflected form of the noun *apple*.
* *Married, marries*, and *marrying* are inflected forms of the verb *marry*.
* *Greener* and *greenest* are inflected forms of the adjective *green*.

Apples, married, marries, marrying, greener, and *greenest* are all examples of inflections. There will be a deeper discussion of the inflections of parts of speech later in this chapter.

For now, let's analyze a single morpheme. We'll look closely at the English morpheme that indicates that a verb is in the past tense. This morpheme is the suffix *–ed*. (For words ending in *e*, this suffix is usually spelled *–d*.) The pronunciation of this suffix depends on the last sound of the root word that the suffix is being added to.

If a word ends with [d] or [t], this past tense suffix is pronounced [ɪd]:

Present tense	Past tense
deed	deeded
heat	heated

If a word ends with a voiced sound other than [d], the past tense suffix is pronounced [d]. As you'll recall, voiced sounds include the vowels and voiced consonants.

Present tense	Past tense
mow	mowed
weigh	weighed
free	freed
blab	blabbed
lag	lagged
buzz	buzzed

If a word ends in a voiceless consonant other than [t], this past tense suffix is pronounced [t]:

Present tense	Past tense
stop	stopped
leak	leaked
muss	mussed

As you can see, the suffix spelled –ed has three pronunciations: [ɪd], [t], and [d]. However, it is the same suffix regardless of which pronunciation is used. You will recall that all suffixes are morphemes. The suffix –ed is a morpheme. Each of the three ways that this morpheme can be pronounced is called an ALLOMORPH. In other words, the phonetic forms [ɪd], [t], and [d] are all allomorphs of the English past-tense morpheme that is spelled –ed.

Something you can do!

You have just learned that the past tense form –ed has three allomorphs. The present-tense form is spelled –s or –es. This form also has three allomorphs. (Examples of this present-tense form are *he passes, she reads*, and *it rusts.*)

There is one pronunciation used with words ending in [s] or [z]. There is another pronunciation for with words ending in voiced sounds (vowels or voiced consonants) other than [z]. There is a third pronunciation used with words ending in voiceless consonants other than [s]. Can you determine what these three allomorphs are? Provide some examples.

The answer can be found at the end of the chapter.

Verbs that form the past tense by adding *–ed* are called REGULAR verbs.

Not all inflectional forms are made by adding an affix. Some are made by changing the form of the base word. For example, the past tense of *drink* is *drank* (not *drinked*). The past tense of *think* is *thought* (not *thinked*). Verbs like *drink* and *think* are called IRREGULAR verbs. The inflections of some irregular verbs form patterns, like *sing/sang/sung* and *sink/sank/sunk*, or *bring/brought* and *think/thought*.

A small number of verbs have very irregular patterns. The verb *be* has many inflections: *am, is, are, was, were, being, been.* In many Indo-European languages, the inflection of the verb meaning "to be" is an exception to the regular inflectional patterns. When you learn these languages, you have to memorize these irregular forms.

(Very rarely, some verb inflections come from an unrelated form. An example of this in English is *go*. Its inflections are *goes, going, went, gone.* The past-tense form *went* is from a form unrelated to the word *go*. An inflected form that is etymologically unrelated to the main word form is called SUPPLETIVE.)

To sum up, inflectional suffixes change the grammatical function of a word. You can make a verb past tense or make a noun plural by adding an inflectional suffix.

3.1.1.2 Derivational affixes

A derivational affix *changes the meaning* of the word.

Earlier in the chapter, we learned about *un–*. Both suffixes that are spelled *un–* are derivational:

- When used as a prefix meaning "not," *un–* is added before certain adjectives to create other adjectives. *Unhappy* means "not happy."
- When used as a prefix to convey reversal or removal, it is used before verbs to create other verbs. *Clog* means "to block movement through something." *Unclog* means "to remove a blockage that is preventing movement through something."

Like *un–*, the addition of some derivational forms results in a word that is the same part of speech:

- When the morpheme *–ish* is added to an adjective, the resulting word is an adjective with the meaning "somewhat." When this suffix is added to the adjective *green*, the result is the adjective *greenish*. *Greenish* means "somewhat green."

Some derivational forms will change the part of speech:

- When the morpheme *–ness* is added to an adjective, the resulting word is a noun with the meaning "the state or condition of having the property referred to by the adjective." When this suffix is added to the adjective *sad*, the resulting word is the noun *sadness*. *Sadness* means "the state of being sad."
- When the morpheme *–fy* (sometimes spelled *–ify*) is added to an adjective, the resulting word is a verb with the meaning "cause to become." When this suffix is added to the adjective *ugly*, the resulting word is the adverb *uglify*. *Uglify* means "to cause to become ugly."
- When the morpheme *–ly* is added to an adjective, the resulting word is an adverb, with the meaning "in the manner of." When this suffix is added to the adjective *sad*, the resulting word is the adverb *sadly*. *Sadly* means "in a sad way."

As shown above, *un–* is an example of two different morphemes that are both derivational and have the same spelling and pronunciation. In contrast, *–er* is an example of two different morphemes, one of which is inflectional and the other is derivational:

- *–er* is an inflectional morpheme when it is added to adjectives: *green/greener*.
- *–er* is a derivational morpheme when it is added to a verb to create a noun meaning "a person who does the activity referred to by the verb": *sing/singer*.

Words can consist of multiple morphemes. The word *misappropriations* consists of:

- *mis–*, a prefix meaning "bad" or "wrong" or "failure";
- the root verb *appropriate*;
- the suffix *–ation*, which is added to verbs to make them into nouns with the meaning of "the action or process of the verb, or the result of that action or process"; and
- the inflectional suffix *–s*, indicating plurality.

Something you can do!

- Read a paragraph from a novel or a news article.
- Break each word in the paragraph into morphemes.
- State whether the morpheme is derivational or inflectional.
- If English is not your first language, do this exercise in your first language. Does your language use more or fewer inflectional and derivational forms than English?

3.2 Inflections by part of speech

Now we'll take a look at inflections associated with parts of speech. Modern English has a very simple system of inflection, so sometimes we'll have to look at other languages for examples of certain inflectional categories. (Refer to section 4.2 for more information about the parts of speech.)

3.2.1 Nouns

For most Indo-European languages, the major inflectional categories for nouns are case, number, and gender. Other categories, such as class, are found in other language families.

3.2.1.1 Case

In many Indo-European languages, nouns change their form by adding a morpheme that indicates the noun's role in the sentence.

Each category of these added morphemes is called a CASE, although this terminology is more common in languages with more categories than English has.

In English, nouns maintain their form in many different roles. For example, "the cat" maintains the form "the cat" in these positions in a sentence:

- subject: *The cat is on the mat.*
- the direct object of a verb: *I petted the cat.*
- the indirect object of a verb: *I gave some food to the cat.*

In English, this basic form is called the NOMINATIVE case.

The POSSESSIVE case indicates ownership. The possessive case is indicated in English by adding the morpheme −'s. When used in this way, *the cat* becomes *the cat's*, as in the sentence *The cat's food is in the cabinet.* (In English, only the nominative and possessive forms of nouns show a distinction. Section 3.2.2 discusses additional forms that English pronouns have.)

Because *the cat* is identical in all of these grammatical roles except for the possessive, word order is very important in English and other languages where grammatical roles aren't indicated with inflections. When different roles are indicated by different case endings, word order is more flexible and serves other functions instead. We'll discuss this further in section 6.7.

Many languages have more endings for nouns than English does. German has four cases. Czech has seven cases. Here are some examples

of the different cases in Czech regarding the word for "cat," used as a
singular noun:

- *kočka* is the form used in the subject position (the NOMINATIVE CASE)
- *kočku* is the form used in the direct object position (the ACCUSA-
  TIVE CASE)
- *kočce* is the form used in the indirect object position (the DATIVE case)

In languages with lots of cases, what we call the possessive in English
is usually called the GENITIVE CASE.

Other languages, like Spanish, have just one nominal case. (NOMI-
NAL is the adjective form of the word *noun*, similar to how ADJECTIVAL
is the adjective form of the word *adjective*.) In English, we can say
the boy's book. In Spanish, you would say *el libro del niño* (literally
"the book of the boy"). Even though Spanish only has one nominal
case, its pronouns have different forms depending on their role in the
sentence. This will be covered in the pronoun section (section 3.2.2).

At the beginning of this section, I referred explicitly to Modern
English. Old English had many more case endings than Modern English.
We'll discuss in the next chapter how the case system in English
changed over the centuries and became more simplified.

3.2.1.2 Number

In English, we distinguish between SINGULAR (referring to one object)
and PLURAL (referring to more than one object). The roles of singular
and plural fall under the category of NUMBER.

The plural forms of most nouns in English are indicated by adding –*s*.

Although these are shown with the letter *s*, phonologically, there are
three different sounds. The pattern is analogous to the pattern that we
examined when discussing the past-tense suffix –*ed* earlier in the chapter.
(An explanation of the three allomorphs of the suffix –*s* is at the end of the
chapter. Even though that description has to do with the verb ending –*s*,
the phonological discussion is the same for this noun suffix –*s*.)

The plural form of most possessive nouns is indicated in writing by
adding an apostrophe to the plural form: *cats'*. Irregular plurals (like
children from *child* or *oxen* from *ox*) show possessive plurals by just
adding –'*s* to the plural form: *children's, oxen's*.

Some languages, such as Arabic, have a DUAL form. The dual is used with two objects. In English, the ending that shows plurality is the same whether you're talking about two cats, five cats, or many cats. In languages with a dual form, there would be a different ending when referring to two cats, in contrast to six cats.

Many Slavic languages (Russian, Polish, Bulgarian, and most other languages of Central and Eastern Europe, except for Hungarian and languages of the Baltic) inflect the noun with the nominative plural form when there are two, three, or four objects and use the genitive plural form with five or more objects.

In languages with a robust case system, there are forms for the plural of each case as well. (Using the Czech word for "cat" again as an example, *kočky* is the nominative and accusative plural form; *kočkám* is the dative plural form.)

3.2.1.3 Gender

In addition to case and number, many languages have different endings for gender. Sometimes the gender can correlate to the actual gender of the referent. For example, the Spanish word *hijo* means "son" and is a masculine word. *Hija*, meaning "daughter," is a feminine word. Usually, though, whether a noun is considered masculine or feminine is arbitrary. Again from Spanish: *la casa* "the house," *la pluma* "the pen," and *la libertad*, "freedom" are feminine. *El perro* "the dog," *el papel* "the paper," and *el barco* "the ship" are masculine. This distinction is maintained in the plural for almost all words, too: *las plumas* "the pens"; *los barcos* "the ships."

Some languages, like German and many of the Slavic languages, also have a third gender, known as NEUTER. In German, *der Hund* "the dog" is masculine, *das Haus* "the house" is neuter, and *die Blume* "the flower" is feminine.

When learning a foreign language that distinguishes gender, you need to memorize the determiner (such as "the" or "that") that accompanies each noun. Although words like "mother" and "father" will usually be feminine and masculine, respectively, across languages, that is not true of all nouns. "The book" is masculine in Spanish (*el libro*), neuter in German (*das Buch*), and feminine in Russian (*эта книга – eta kniga*).[1]

In English, gender is relegated to a few forms that specifically refer to the gender of the referent. For example, *–ess* was once commonly used to show the feminine form of words, like *actor/actress*, *governor/governess*, and *prince/princess*. In many cases, like *sculptress*, *stewardess*, or *poetess*, the form is usually considered sexist and should be avoided. Other feminine suffixes include *–trix*: *aviator/aviatrix*, *executor/executrix*. In Middle English, *–stere* was a feminine form; it is now seen only in *spinster* – literally, "a woman who spins thread." All other uses of *–ster* (like *hipster, scenester*, and *fraudster*) derive from *–stere* but are not gender specific.

3.2.1.4 Class

The forms described above are all features of Indo-European languages. They are, of course, not the only examples of inflectional affixation. One important inflectional category outside of the Indo-European languages is CLASS, which is found in Bantu languages, for example. Whereas Indo-European gender consists of two or three categories, many Bantu languages have around 20 classes, each with its own prefix marker.

Some nouns are grouped into classes by function, shape, or other common attributes. Similar to gender, sometimes the categorization is arbitrary.[2]

3.2.2 Pronouns

English pronouns have more forms than nouns do.

Words like *I* and *she* are used in the subject position; these are said to be in the nominative case. (*I am happy. She is going to work.*)

As the direct object of a verb or as the object of a preposition, you would use *me* and *her*; these are said to be in the OBJECTIVE case. (*Tom thanked me. Anna gave the paper to her.*)

The possessive forms are *my* or *mine* and *her* or *hers*. These are said to be in the possessive case (which is also called the genitive case in certain languages). (*My head hurts. Those books are mine. Her dog is barking. That house is hers.*)

3.2.3 Adjectives

There are two inflections associated with adjectives in English: the COMPARATIVE and the SUPERLATIVE. Each is formed in one of two ways.

To make the comparative, for most words of one syllable and some words of two or more syllables, you add the form –er. For most words of two or more syllables, you place the word *more* before it.

red/redder	happy/happier
dangerous/more dangerous	interested/more interested

To make the superlative, for most words of one syllable and some words of two or more syllables, you add the form –est. For most words of two or more syllables, you place the word *most* before it:

red/reddest	happy/happiest
dangerous/most dangerous	interested/most interested

A small number of English adjectives have irregular forms:

bad	*worse*	*worst*
good	*better*	*best*

3.2.4 Verbs

English has relatively few morphemes that are associated with verbs to indicate number, person, or tense.

In the simple present tense, most verbs have the same form as the INFINITIVE. (The infinitive form is the one used in the construction with the word "to": *to bake, to swim, to run.*)

In the present tense, with the exception of *to be* and *to have*, English verbs share the same form for first-person singular and plural, second-person singular and plural, and third-person plural. The third-person singular is made by adding [z] to words ending in voiceless consonants and vowels, [s] to words ending in voiced consonants, and [ɪz] to words ending with [s], [z], [ʃ], [ʒ], [tʃ], or [dʒ].[3] In terms of spelling, this usually means adding –s at the end of the word, or –es if the word ends in s, z, x, sh, or ch.

	Singular	Plural
First person	I wait	we wait
	I itch	we itch
Second person	you wait	you wait
	you itch	you itch
Third person	he, she, it wait**s**	they wait
	he, she, it itch**es**	they itch

This ending, written as –s or –es, is a morpheme that indicates the third-person singular.

Collectively, the forms shown above are called the CONJUGATION of the verb. As mentioned, a couple verbs have complex conjugations. *To be* and *to have* are examples:

	Singular	Plural
First person	I am	we are
Second person	you are	you are
Third person	he, she, it is	they are

	Singular	Plural
First person	I have	we have
Second person	you have	you have
Third person	he, she, it has	they have

Additionally, there is a pronunciation shift for the third-person singular of *to do*. *Does* is pronounced [dəz], not [doz].

Compare this approach to languages where number and person are indicated with endings, like Spanish *esperar* (which means "to wait" or "to hope").

	Singular	Plural
First person	(yo) esper**o**	(nosotros) esper**amos**
Second person	(tú) esper**as**	(vosotros) esper**aís**
Third person	(él, ella, Usted) esper**a**	(Ustedes) esper**an**[4]

One result of having different morphemes that show number and person is that the use of pronouns in such languages are usually optional. *Esperamos* can only mean "we wait." *Espero* means "I wait." In English, because *wait* is used with *I, you, we,* and *they,* we must say *I wait, you wait,* and so forth.

In Spanish, all infinitives end in *–ar, –er,* or *–ir*. The above chart shows endings for verbs whose infinitive ends in *–ar*. There are different endings for verbs ending in *–er* and *–ir*.

As noted earlier in this chapter, the past tense and past participle of most English verbs are formed by adding [d] to words ending in voiceless consonants and vowels, [t] to words ending in voiced consonants, and [ɪd] to words ending with [t] or [d]. In terms of spelling, this usually means adding *–ed* at the end of the word, or *–d* if the word ends in *e*. Such verbs are called regular verbs and include *to call, to bike, to move,* and *to substantiate.*

Several dozen verbs in English, mostly of Germanic origin, show past tense by instead changing the vowel sound in the middle, sometimes in addition to adding a [t] sound at the end. Such verbs are called irregular verbs and include *to buy, to bring, to sink,* and *to sing.*

Highly inflected languages have separate forms for the past tense. This table gives the simple past tense in Spanish for a verb whose infinitive form ends in *–ar*: *esperar,* meaning "to wait":

	Singular	*Plural*
First person	(yo) esper**é**	(nosotros) esper**amos**
Second person	(tú) esper**aste**	(vosotros) esper**asteís**
Third person	(él, ella, Usted) esper**ó**	(Ustedes) esper**aron**

The future tense in English is even more straightforward. The word *will* is placed between the subject and the verb: *I will go. He will go.* In languages like Spanish, there is yet another pattern of conjugations.

There are many other sets of endings that verbs can take to impart different tenses. In English, these grammatical phenomena are indicated by words instead of inflectional endings. For example, *would* and *could* indicate conditional uses (*would eat, could eat.*) The belief that something is true or likely is indicated by words like *may* or *might* (*may eat, might eat*).

The formation of some tenses involves the use of words and inflectional endings: *I am eating*, *she was eating*, *we had eaten*, *we will have eaten*. In many other languages, these uses are represented with different inflectional endings, so that a single verb can have dozens (or hundreds) of endings.

Languages that have complex systems of conjugation and declensions are much freer in word order. Languages that don't distinguish these categories with morphological features are more bound to a specific word order. This subject, and the ramifications of this tendency, will be addressed in the next chapter.

The morphology of a language changes very slowly over time. The complex endings of verb conjugations or noun declensions might simplify – this happened in the progression from Old English to Modern English. Nonetheless, there are noteworthy phenomena in English worth discussing.

3.3 Change in morphology over time

In Chapter 2, you learned that the phonology of a language can change during the course of a person's lifetime.

In contrast, changes to morphology don't happen very often. There is a great deal of evidence for variation within a language, such as *I ain't* versus *I'm not* or *I saw* versus *I seen*. And although a speaker of a variety of English considered to be less prestigious can learn forms that are considered standard, the morphology of each variety of English is very stable.

Changes in morphology happen far less frequently than changes in phonology.

3.3.1 Verb paradigms from Old English to Modern English

As mentioned, Old English had a much more robust system of verb conjugation and noun declension. Here's a comparison of the conjugation of "to have" in Old English, Middle English, and Modern English:

Old English[5]

	Singular	Plural
First person	ic hæbbe	we habbaþ
Second person	þu hæfst or hafast	ge habbaþ
Third person	he, hit, heo hæfþ or hafaþ	hie habbaþ

Middle English

	Singular	Plural
First person	I have	we haveth or haven
Second person	thou hast	you haveth or haven
Third person	he, she, it hath	they haveth or haven

Early Modern English

	Singular	Plural
First person	I have	we have
Second person	thou hast	you have
Third person	he, she, it hath	they have

Modern English

	Singular	Plural
First person	I have	we have
Second person	you have	you have
Third person	he, she, it has	they have

As you can see, over the centuries, the multiple present tense forms have simplified. There are some varieties of English spoken today where the conjugation has simplified further and *has* is the only present form.

3.3.2 The loss of thou

Earlier in the chapter, where we discussed the Spanish conjugation of *esperar* "wait," in the singular column, you'll see *tú* and *Usted*. *Tú* is the informal form of singular "you," used with family and friends. *Usted* is the formal form. (Verbs with *tú* are conjugated with second-person forms, and verbs with *Usted* are conjugated with third-person forms.)

English used to have different forms for singular and plural *you* (*thou* and *you*, respectively), as seen in the tables above.

You'll still see *thou* used in certain versions of the Bible and in the works of Shakespeare and his contemporaries in the early days of Modern English. English speakers eventually stopped using *thou* in favor of *you* outside of religious contexts and a couple of idioms.

The verbs associated with *thou* had an ending different from the other forms: *thou art, thou didst, thou mayest, thou hadst* – generally ending in *–est* or *–st*. (Like other forms of "to be," *thou art* is an exception.)

3.3.3 –ly dropping

A more contemporary example is the loss of the derivational suffix *–ly* that is added to adjectives to make adverbs. Perhaps you'll recall the ad campaign for Apple computers: "Think different."

In recent decades, there are a multitude of citations that show this suffix being dropped. The result of dropping *–ly* is that words that look like the adjective form are being used as adverbs. While some people criticize this change, it is becoming more and more common. Perhaps in another several decades, adverbs ending in *–ly* will seem as quaint as *thou* does to modern speakers, and English will have undergone a morphological shift.

3.3.4 Third-person singular pronouns and the gender binary

People often use *they* as a singular pronoun when the gender of the referent is unknown or not specified, as in *Everyone took their hat and left*. Although some consider this to be a violation of English grammar, this use of *they* has been in existence for centuries. (Singular *they* will be discussed further in section 8.2.5.)

Singular *they* is also used by people who do not conform to the gender binary, those who identify as neither male nor female. However, the pronouns *they/them* are not the only pronouns that genderfluid people have advocated. Among the more common ones are *xe/xem, ze/hir,* and *ze/zir.* It is very difficult for an intentionally constructed word to become assimilated into a language, and on that basis, *they/them* has an advantage over the other forms. Time will tell which form becomes the predominant third-person singular form to refer to a person who does not conform to the gender binary. We are witnessing the development of a morphological change.

3.4 Conclusion

In this chapter, we've looked at the morphemes that make up English words. We've looked at the difference between derivational and inflectional morphemes and the role they play in changing the forms of words or making new words. We've also looked at how these forms have changed over time.[6] In the next chapter, we'll be looking more closely at parts of speech and the roles they play in the structure of sentences.

3.5 Questions for discussion

- Describe how the following prefixes or suffixes affect base words that they're added to: *–like, un–, –er, –ed.*
- Describe the differences between derivational morphemes and inflectional morphemes.
- If the nouns of a language don't have many case endings, like in English, what effect does that have on the order of words in a sentence?
- If you speak a language other than English, compare the conjugation of verbs between the two languages.

Answer to the question from section 3.1.1.1

Here's the answer to the first **Something you can do!** question in this chapter. This question asked you to come up with the allomorphs for the present tense form *–s/–es.*

If a word ends with [s], [z], [ʃ], [ʒ], [tʃ], or [dʒ],[7] this past-tense suffix is pronounced [ɪz]:

Base form	Third-person singular, present tense
place	places
blaze	blazes
lash	lashes
catch	catches
wedge	wedges

If a word ends with a voiced sound other than [z], [ʒ], or [dʒ], the past-tense suffix is pronounced [z]. As you'll recall, a voiced sound includes the vowels and voiced consonants.

Base form	Third-person singular, present tense
mow	mows
weigh	weighs
free	frees
blab	blabs
lag	lags
need	needs

If a word ends in a voiceless consonant other than [s], [ʃ], or [tʃ], the past-tense suffix is pronounced [s].

Base form	Third-person singular, present tense
stop	stops
peak	peaks
fret	frets

The phonetic forms [ɪz], [z], and [s] are all allomorphs of the English third-person singular present-tense morpheme spelled –s or –es.

These sound changes are the same for the plural forms of regular nouns, too.

Notes

1 Russian is written in a different alphabet (called the Cyrillic alphabet). When showing words that use different alphabets, like Russian or Greek, this book will also give the TRANSLITERATION – that is, how the letters in the other alphabet would be written in the Roman alphabet. For example, the sound [n] is written in English as 'n' and in Russian as 'н.'

2 Further Reading: Derek Nurse and Gérard Philippson (editors), *The Bantu Languages*.

3 [ʃ] is the "sh" sound of **sh**ut. [ʒ] is the "zh" sound of plea**s**ure. [tʃ] is the "ch" sound of **ch**at. [dʒ] is the "j" or "dg" sound of **judge**. [ʒ] doesn't appear at the end of many English words; one example would be the informal abbreviation of *casual* as *cazh*.

4 *yo* = *I*, tú = the familiar form of singular *you*, *él* = *he, ella* = *she, Usted* = the formal form of singular *you*, *nosotros* = *we, vosotros* = the familiar form of plural *you, Ustedes* = the formal form of plural *you*.

5 The symbols æ and þ are explained on page 5 of this book. Further Reading: Peter S. Baker, *Introduction to Old English*.

6 Further Reading: Martin Haspelmath and Andrea Sims, *Understanding Morphology*.

7 See endnote 3 (this chapter) for an explanation of [ʃ], [ʒ], [tʃ], and [dʒ].

Chapter 4

Sentence structure

4.0 Introduction

In earlier chapters, we examined how to combine sounds to form syllables and words.

You can put words together to form phrases, clauses, and sentences. SYNTAX refers to the structure of the phrases, clauses, and sentences in a language and the rules that govern how they're structured.

In this chapter we will examine:

- the structure of sentences, phrases, and clauses
- the categorization of words by part of speech
- the categorization of sentence structures
- how words can combine in English
- how English syntax has changed over time
- how English syntax varies from region to region

4.1 Sentences, clauses, and phrases

As you will recall from Chapter 2, you can produce a string of sounds (like *glorpee*) that is pronounceable but has no meaning in a given language. There are strings (like *vzcvrnkls*) that violate the phonotactics of one language but not another. There are strings (like *lrgbfmg*) that violate phonotactics universally.

Similarly, some strings of words form sentences in a language. There are many more examples of strings of words that do not form sentences. First we'll examine sentence structure according to traditional English grammar.

4.1.1 Sentences

A SENTENCE has a *subject* and a *predicate*. It is an independent unit.

A SUBJECT is a noun or a noun phrase that shows who or what (i) is doing the action of the sentence or (ii) is described by the predicate. In English, sentences that are commands often omit the subject. In most cases, the subject of a command is *you*, as in the command *Run quickly!* Commands like *Run quickly* are considered sentences, and the subject is said to be UNDERSTOOD. (Nouns and noun phrases are explained in section 4.2.1.)

A PREDICATE modifies the subject. The predicate includes everything that comes after the subject: the verb and the objects and other phrases associated with the verb. We say that the verb GOVERNS these objects and phrases, which are sometimes called COMPLEMENTS. (Verbs are explained in section 4.2.2.)

In the following sentences, the subject is in *italics* and the predicate is in regular text.

> *The dog* ran toward the fence.
> *She* gave her friend a present for his birthday.
> *The man in the red cape* is a famous magician.
> *Honesty* is the best policy.

4.1.2 Clauses

A CLAUSE also has a subject and a predicate. An INDEPENDENT CLAUSE (also called a MAIN CLAUSE) is a sentence.

A DEPENDENT CLAUSE is part of a complex sentence and is not (as the name implies) an independent unit. That is, it can't stand alone. Let's make an analogy to morphology. The suffix *–ment* has meaning: it is added to verbs to indicate an action or process. *Discernment* is the action of discerning. Yet, *–ment* doesn't stand alone as a word. Similarly, a dependent clause has meaning but does not constitute a sentence itself.

In the sentence *I spoke to the man who sat in the corner*, the sequence of words *who sat in the corner* is a dependent clause. It has a subject (*who*) and a predicate (*sat in the corner*), but is part of the larger sentence. Although the question *Who sat in the corner?* is a complete sentence, this same string of words, when used as a statement, is not. In spoken English, you can discern a question from a statement because the voice rises and falls differently in each case. (Say *Who sat in the corner?* and *I spoke to the man who sat in the corner* aloud. You will hear this difference.)

When the word *clause* is used in contrast to *sentence*, it usually is shorthand for *dependent clause.*

4.1.3 Phrases

A PHRASE is a sequence of words that have meaning as a group within that sentence. In the sentence *She gave her friend a present for his birthday*, the sequences *her friend, a present*, and *for his birthday* are all phrases.

A sentence, clause, or phrase is said to be well-formed if it follows the grammatical rules of that language. Similar to how *lrgbfmg* does not follow the phonological patterns of English, the sequence *Ball fuzzy the the eat actually twenty-five snored by in proudly an with* does not follow the syntactic patterns of English. Just as *glorpee* follows phonological patterns of English but has no obvious meaning, you can construct sentences that follow the syntactic patterns of English but have no coherent, straightforward meaning. (One of the most famous examples of such a sentence is from the linguist Noam Chomsky: *Colorless green ideas sleep furiously.*)

Kinds of phrases include noun phrases, verb phrases, and prepositional phrases. These are explained below.

4.2 Parts of speech

The notion of the PART OF SPEECH will make it easier to analyze how words group together to form sentence, clauses, and phrases. You probably encountered the parts of speech in your elementary-school education. It's commonly taught that there are seven or eight parts of speech in English, and most dictionaries follow that arrangement, too.

These categories are the same ones used in the study of Latin and Greek. In English (which, unlike Latin and Greek, is a Germanic language), not every word is neatly accommodated by this system. But for the purpose of discussing the roles of words within a sentence, they come in handy.

Of course, many words can be classified as different parts of speech depending on how they're used in a sentence. *Table*, for example, can be used both as a noun and a verb. These two definitions are from the *American Heritage Dictionary*:

> *noun*: A piece of furniture usually supported by one or more legs and having a flat top surface on which objects can be placed.
> *verb*: To postpone consideration of (a piece of legislation, for example).

Many nouns can also be used attributively in a role similar to that of adjectives. *Brick* is a noun. In the phrase *brick wall*, *brick* is still a noun – although here its function is like that of an adjective.

Let's take a look at the basic parts of speech and a few related key concepts regarding syntax. We'll start with the basic building blocks of sentences: nouns and verbs. Together, these two categories constitute the bulk of English vocabulary.[1]

4.2.1 Nouns

You might have been taught that "a noun is a person, place, or thing." This simple definition is almost sufficient for our discussion, but it is not an exhaustive inventory of what nouns can be. Qualities and actions, for example, are also nouns.

person	Abigail Adams	Howard Hughes
	doctor	sister
	neighbor	Spaniard
place	Omaha	Newfoundland
	floodplain	jungle
	zoo	museum

thing	rock	paper
	potato	frame
	necklace	blood
quality	freedom	liberty
	independence	sadness
	sincerity	insecurity
action	participation	enunciation
	intensification	action

Nouns serve several different functions in sentences:

as the subject of a verb:	The *child* laughs.
	The *park* is open.
	The *dog* swims.
	The *rain* falls.
	Pudding is delicious.
	Your *honesty* is welcome.
	The *negotiations* are finished.
as the object of a verb:	Javi hugged his *cousin*.
	Andra painted the *wall*.
	I flew to *Chicago*.
	The drought brought *misery*.
as object of a preposition:	I gave the ball to *Shelly*.
	Fallon lives in *Baltimore*.
	The ring is made of *metal*.
	The host treated us with *kindness*.

Nouns in English, as you will recall from the last chapter, can be inflected to show number (singular or plural). Possession is shown with – *s*. If you can add – *s* to a word to indicate possession, it's probably a noun.

A NOUN PHRASE is a phrase that functions as a noun in a sentence. A noun phrase includes a noun and any adjectives, determiners, or other modifiers that are attached to it. In the sentence *Tom ate pizza*, *Tom* is the subject. You could also say *My friend in the striped shirt ate pizza*. *My friend in the striped shirt* is a noun phrase. In fact, it is a noun phrase that exists of a shorter noun phrase (*My friend*) and a prepositional phrase (*in the striped shirt*). (Prepositional phrases are explained in section 4.2.7.)

4.2.2 Verbs

Verbs express existence, occurrence, or action:

existence	be	*action*	run
	seem		walk
occurrence	think		wash
	appear		

You can categorize verbs by what kind of nouns or noun phrases occur with them. These categorizations involve whether or not a verb "takes an object." First, let's examine what that means.

Most simple sentences consist of two primary components: a subject and a predicate.

The subject is represented by a noun, pronoun, or noun phrase. Typically, it denotes who or what the sentence is about. The predicate includes everything following the subject, including the verb and the objects governed by the verb.

Subject	Predicate
The ball	is blue and round.
She	bought a new house last week.
My cousins	came to my birthday party.
The clown with the red nose	gave the man in the mask a large pie.

A TAG QUESTION follows a statement and is used to confirm that statement. In *The ball is blue and round, isn't it?* the question *isn't it?* is a tag question. Tag questions can help you easily determine the subject. The pronoun in the tag question always refers to the subject and can be substituted for the subject. *The ball is blue and round, isn't it? Yes, it is blue and round.* Therefore, the subject is *the ball.*

There are noun phrases and prepositional phrases that are associated with the verb. In the clown example (*The clown with the red nose gave the man in the mask a large pie.*), associated with the verb *gave*, the phrase *the man in the mask* answers the question "Who was the recipient of the giving?" and the phrase *a large pie* answers the question "What was given?" We say that the verb *governs*, or *takes*, these phrases. These phrases that are governed by the verbs are called OBJECTS.

So, verbs are categorized by whether they govern objects or not.

Verbs that don't govern any objects are called INTRANSITIVE VERBS. (In dictionaries, intransitive verbs are marked with abbreviations like *iv, vi*, or *intr.v.*) Examples of verbs that are used intransitively include:

- *sleep*, as in *I am sleeping.*
- *run*, as in *He runs every day after work.*
- *defrost*, as in *After the windows defrost, we can see through them.*

In the *run* example, you might be wondering about "every day after work." This phrase is not an object of the verb. Rather, it is an adverb phrase that modifies (that is, limits the meaning of) the verb. Adverbs, as you will see below, often explain when, how, or where the action of the verb occurs.

Other verbs take one or more noun phrases as objects. The noun phrases that follow these verbs are called DIRECT OBJECTS. These verbs are called TRANSITIVE VERBS. (In dictionaries, transitive verbs are marked with abbreviations like *tv, vt*, or *tr.v.*) Examples of transitive verbs include:

- *sing*, as in *We sang an Italian song.*
- *found*, as in *I found a dollar on the sidewalk.*
- *carry*, as in *She carried a backpack.*

Many verbs have both transitive and intransitive senses:

| *sing* | intransitive: | *We sang for an hour.* |
| | transitive: | *We sang Latin hymns.* |

| *defrost* | intransitive: | *These windows defrost automatically.* |
| | transitive: | *The driver defrosted the windows.* |

Some verbs can also take INDIRECT OBJECTS. In the sentence *She gave the child a present*, "a present" is the direct object and "the child" is the indirect object. Such verbs are said to be DITRANSITIVE VERBS. Many dictionaries for learners of English will indicate that verbs are ditransitive; most dictionaries for fluent speakers define these senses within the list of transitive definitions.

Sometimes the indirect object is represented by a prepositional phrase. The sentence *She gave the child a present* can also be expressed as *She gave a present to the child*.

Phrases that occur with verbs in the predicate of a sentence are known as the complements of the verb. These complements include the direct objects, indirect objects, prepositional phrases, and adverbial phrases. In the sentence *They drove the car down the road to the store*, "the car," "down the road," and "to the store" are all complements of the verb *drove*.

A VERB PHRASE is a phrase that consists of a verb (called a MAIN VERB) and any AUXILIARY VERBS that accompany it. One set of auxiliary verbs are known as MODAL VERBS. In English they are: *can/could, may/might, must, will/would*, and *shall/should*. The other auxiliary verbs are *have, do*, and *be* (and their inflections), when used in conjunction with verbs to form different tenses. In the following verb phrases, the bold word is the main verb, and the other words are its auxiliary verbs:

*did **eat***
*had **traveled***
*were **dancing***
*has been **listening***
*might have been **laughing***
*should be **sleeping***

4.2.3 Adjectives

Adjectives MODIFY nouns. Here, *modify* means that an adjective describes the noun it is associated with or limits the range of potential nouns that are referred to. In the phrase *a gray cat*, "gray" describes the cat – it is gray in color. It limits our concept of "cat" by eliminating reference to black cats, white cats, and so on. Adjectives also function as part of the predicate when they follow a form of *be* (or another linking verb), as in *The cat was gray*.

In English, adjectives typically precede the noun (a *pink* flower); adjectives can follow the noun too, although the effect is often poetic (a morning both *cloudy* and *dreary*). This placement is language specific. In Spanish, for example, adjectives generally follow the noun: *la casa blanca* (literally, "the house white").

Adjectives can be expressed in degrees. The use of the suffix *–er* or the word *more* (*sweeter, louder, more important, more frenzied*) is called the COMPARATIVE degree. The use of the suffix *–est* or the word *most* (*happiest, greenest, most intense, most vitriolic*) is called the SUPERLATIVE degree.

4.2.4 Adverbs

Adverbs modify verbs, adjectives, or other adverbs. These include words of time, manner, or place. As such, they often answer the question when, how, or where something is done.

adverbs of time:	I *often* go to the beach.
	She *never* eats meat.
	He *always* exercises in the evening.
	It's raining *now*.
adverbs of manner:	It was hard to hear him because he spoke *softly*.
	He acted *indifferently* when I explained the problem.
	She sang "Happy Birthday" *exuberantly*.
adverbs of place:	Put the boxes *here*.
	I want to go *there*.
	The cat is *nowhere* to be found.

Many adverbs can be formed by adding the suffix *–ly* to an adjective:

happy	happily
loud	loudly

4.2.5 Pronouns

Pronouns stand in for nouns or noun phrases. They're used so that you don't have to repeat the same noun or noun phrase. Instead of saying "My oldest brother came over for a visit yesterday. When my oldest brother arrived, I gave my oldest brother an iced tea," you can replace most instances of "my oldest brother" with a pronoun. Unless the person being discussed has been established earlier in the conversation, you'll still use the full phrase in the first occurrence, so that your audience knows who you're referring to: "My oldest brother came over for a visit yesterday. When *he* arrived, I gave *him* an iced tea."

As you see in the above example, in English, pronouns take different forms depending on the role they play in a sentence to a much greater degree than nouns do. Compare these sentences:

> *The woman* stood in line.
> Angie asked *the woman* for directions.
> This apple belongs to the *woman*.

The same form, *woman*, is used for the subject position and object position. Now let's look at the pronouns:

> *She* stood in line.
> Angie asked *her* for directions.
> This apple belongs to *her*.

The subject position uses a different form (*she*) than the object position (*her*).

Singular possessive nouns are formed with *–'s*. The corresponding pronoun has no apostrophe:

> This car is *the woman's*.
> This car is *hers*.

(When used before a noun (*her car, his wallet, their proposal*), these forms are classified as an adjective.)

So, for example, the first-person singular pronoun has a different form in the subject, object, possessive, and reflexive positions:

> *I* can run a mile in eight minutes.
> My parents gave *me* a book for my birthday.
> Those car keys are *mine*.
> I bought *myself* a new phone.

The list of pronouns in English is small and contained, and easy to list.

	Subject	*Object*	*Possessive*	*Reflexive*
First-person singular	I	me	mine	myself
Second-person singular	you	you	yours	yourself
Third-person masculine singular	he	him	his	himself
Third-person feminine singular	she	her	hers	herself
Third-person nonbinary singular	they	them	theirs	themself
Third-person neuter singular	it	it	its	itself
First-person plural	we	us	ours	ourselves
Second-person plural	you	you	yours	yourselves
Third-person plural	they	them	theirs	themselves

The pronouns in subject position are *I, you, he, she, it, we*, and *they*. As objects of verbs and prepositions, pronouns take the forms *me, you, him, her, it, us*, and *them*. To indicate possession after a form of be, they take the form *mine, yours, his, hers, its, ours*, and *theirs*. The reflexive form is *myself, yourself, himself, herself, themself* (discussed at the end of this section), *itself, ourselves, yourselves, themselves.*

Nouns and verbs come and go in the language over the course of decades or even years, but the pronouns don't change that frequently. In almost all varieties of English, the use of *thou* and its forms (*thee, thine, thyself*) as a singular second-person form dropped out several centuries ago, replaced by *you*.

Much more recently, the use of *they* as a singular, gender-neutral pronoun (which has been a feature of English for centuries) has also been adopted as a pronoun for people who do not conform to the gender binary. This, in turn, has given rise to the pronoun *themself* as the singular reflexive form. Although some people bristle at this form because it has been taught as a nonstandard form, this construction is analogous to the singular form of *yourself*, in contrast to the plural form *yourselves*. Similarly, singular *they* takes a plural verb, much in the same way singular *you* takes a plural verb. The fact that there is an outcry over the recent acceptance of this feature (which, again, is several centuries old) is more proof that even something as relatively static as a language's pronoun system can undergo change. (There is further discussion about singular *they* in section 8.2.5.)

4.2.6 Articles and determiners

An ARTICLE is used to specify a noun. In English, articles are either definite or indefinite.

The DEFINITE ARTICLE in English is *the*.

The INDEFINITE ARTICLE in English is either *a* or *an*. *A* is used when the following word begins with consonant sound. *An* is used when the following word begins with a vowel sound.

The definite article is used when the noun has a fixed identity, in context. The indefinite article is used when the noun does not have a fixed identity. For example, when discussing your neighbor and her dog, you might say, *My neighbor has a dog. The dog is a terrier*. In the first reference, *dog* is used with *a* because there was no previous reference to the dog in the discourse. The later reference to *the dog* uses *the* because *the dog* now has a fixed reference. There are, of course, many other uses for *the* versus *a*.

Many languages (Russian, for example) lack articles. For native speakers of a language that does not have articles, learning the nuances of articles in a foreign language is one of the harder parts of acquiring that language.

DETERMINERS are a subset of words that modify nouns. This category includes the articles, possessive adjectives (*her, his, its, theirs, my, our*), demonstrative adjectives (*that, this, these, those*), and certain other adjectives, like *any* and *both*. What sets determiners apart from other adjectives is that they must occur first in a noun phrase:

the last large marble	never	*last large the marble*
her big red car	never	*big red her car*
that smelly old sock	never	*smelly old that sock*
any random interesting fact	never	*random interesting any fact*

4.2.7 Prepositions

PREPOSITIONS are words that are usually placed before nouns and relate those nouns to other nouns, adjectives, or verbs. Examples include *in, to, from, by, with*:

- The gift is *in* the box.
- I gave the gift *to* my brother.
- This book is *from* Canada.
- I wrote my signature *with* a pen.

In some languages, words that serve this function follow nouns instead of preceding nouns. In this context, they are sometimes referred to as POSTPOSITIONS. For example, the Japanese words for the prepositions "from" and "to" are *kara* and *e*, respectively. The Japanese translation of the sentence "Masako goes from Tokyo to Boston" is *Masako ga Tōkyō kara Bosuton e iku.* As postpositions, *kara* and *e* are placed after the noun they are associated with. (*Ga* is a particle that is placed after the subject of the sentence. *Iku* translates as "goes.")

In other languages, certain positional attributes are reflected by using a different ending for the noun. In Finnish, for example, prepositions typically do not stand alone. The singular nominative form of the word "house" in Finnish is *talo*. The Finnish word for "in the house" is *talossa*, "into the house" is *taloonsa*, and "from the house" is *talolta.*

In English, a PREPOSITIONAL PHRASE consists of a preposition followed by a noun, pronoun, or noun phrase. In the following sentences, the prepositional phrases are italicized:

- The room was decorated *with balloons.*
- My suitcase is *behind me.*
- I walked *to the park.*

4.2.8 Conjunctions

A CONJUNCTION is a word that connects two or more words, phrases, or sentences. In English, they don't take affixes or inflectional endings. There are three main kinds of conjunctions: coordinating, correlative, and subordinating.

COORDINATING CONJUNCTIONS join words with words, phrases with phrases, and clauses with clauses within a sentence. Words that are connected by a coordinating conjunction belong to the same part of speech. In English, the coordinating conjunctions are *and, but, or, nor, for, yet*, and *so*:

with words:	You can have *milk **or** soda.* (nouns)
	You can *run **or** jog.* (verbs)
	Are you *happy **or** sad*? (adjectives)
with phrases:	I have *a big red book **and** a small blue book.*
with clauses:	*I went to the store, **but** the store was closed.*

CORRELATIVE CONJUNCTIONS occur in pairs, but not next to each other. They connect words with words, phrases with phrases, and clauses with clauses within a sentence. Words connected by correlative conjunctions belong to the same part of speech. In English, correlative conjunctions include *either . . . or, neither . . . nor, both . . . and*, and *not only . . . but also*.

with words:	You can have ***either** milk **or** soda.*
with phrases:	I have ***both** a big red book **and** a small blue book.*
with clauses:	***Not only** did I go to the store, **but also** I went to the library.*

A SUBORDINATING CONJUNCTION is used to signal the beginning of a subordinating clause. Such a clause cannot stand alone as a sentence. It must be connected to an independent clause. For example, in the sentence *If you leave before 8:00, you will be able to catch the bus*, the word *if* is a subordinating conjunction. *If you leave before 8:00* cannot stand alone as a sentence. It is connected to the independent clause *you will be able to catch the bus*. Other subordinating conjunctions in English include *although*, *because*, *unless*, *when*, and *while*.

In English, prepositions, conjunctions, and articles don't take affixes or inflectional endings. The members of these categories are sometimes collectively referred to as FUNCTION WORDS.

4.2.9 Interjections

INTERJECTIONS are words that express emotion. Often they stand alone as a sentence. Or, in the words of the *Schoolhouse Rock* videos of the 1970s, "They're generally set apart from a sentence by an exclamation point, or by a comma when the feeling's not as strong."[2] Examples include:

Hey! Watch where you're going!
Ow! I stubbed my toe.
Wow, you're really on the ball today.

Something you can do!

- What part of speech do these words belong to? If you're unsure, consult a dictionary. Some of these belong to multiple parts of speech.

dog	under	faint	the
blue	happily	construct	hey
snow	light	of	my

- Create:

  - A list of five words that are only used as nouns.
  - A list of five words that are only used as verbs.
  - A list of five words that are only used as adjectives.

> Was this task easy or difficult? What made it easy or difficult?
>
> • Compare your list with classmates to see if they agree that these words can only be categorized in these parts of speech or not.
> • If you speak a language other than English, do the same exercise in that language. Was it easier to do, or harder? Why do you think that might be?

4.2.10 Parts of speech changing over time

Some parts of speech change very little over time. Within the Modern English period, prepositions, conjunctions, and articles have barely changed at all.

As noted in the pronoun section (section 4.2.5), *thou* and its forms have fallen into disuse. *They* and its related forms have actually been used as a singular form (as in *Everyone took their hat and left*) for centuries, but a more recent innovation is its use with a person who does not conform to the gender binary. Invented pronouns (such as *xe* or *ze*) have not been as quick to catch on for nonbinary use, in part because *they* has been used as a singular pronoun for so long.

In section 3.4.3, we discussed the tendency for the *–ly* of adverbs to be dropped, as in Apple's famous campaign "Think different." Aside from that shift, relatively few new adverbs have been added to the language – the bulk of new words are nouns or verbs. New nouns and verbs enter the language with great frequency, as do adjectives to a lesser degree.

Parts of speech can be turned into other parts of speech by adding certain suffixes. As noted by Calvin in Bill Watterson's comic strip *Calvin and Hobbes*: "Verbing weirds language."[3]

A word belonging to one part of speech can come to be used as a different part of speech. This is a significant agent of change in English, which is comparatively more fluid when it comes to using words in multiple roles. (In most Indo-European languages, verbs have specific endings: for example, all Spanish verbs end in *–ar*, *–er*, or *–ir*, and it would be odd to use a verb form as a noun. Not so in English!)

Often there's resistance when verbs begin to be used as nouns. *Ask* is a verb, but people in the business and fundraising worlds will use *ask* as a noun to mean "the thing that you're asking for" or *spend* to refer to "the amount that you're going to spend for something." The use of *friend* as a verb only recently became prevalent through its use in social media; prior to that, *friend* was primarily used as a noun. (The *Oxford English Dictionary* defines several obsolete and rare senses of *friend* as a verb.) Over time, these changes begin to sound normal.

It might surprise you that the use of now common verbs aggravated many people when these words were first used as verbs, like the use of *contact* as a verb (*She contacted me to schedule an appointment*). People were advised to use a specific verb: *She telephoned me, She sent me a letter*, etc. (See also section 8.2.5.) Similarly, the use of *impact* as a verb (*This donation will impact our ability to help the poor* versus *This donation will have an impact on our ability to help the poor*) became acceptable only relatively recently; even now, some criticize its use as a verb without a direct object. This note, last revised in 2015, from the *American Heritage Dictionary* shows the trajectory of the acceptance of *impact*'s different roles:

> *Impact* in the figurative sense of "a dramatic effect" came under criticism in the 1960s, both as a noun and verb. Complaints that the noun was a pointless hyperbole and a vogue word turned out to be short-lived, and this usage is now is standard: in our 2015 survey, 97 percent of the Usage Panel accepted *The program might have a positive impact on our nation's youth.* (A similar sentence was accepted by 93 percent of the Panel in 2001.) The verb is a different matter. Many people dislike it because they assume it was converted from the noun in the manner of voguish and bureaucratic words like *dialogue* and *interface*, but in fact *impact* was a verb long before it was a noun – the verb dates from the early 1600s, the noun from the late 1700s. Most of the Panelists

still disapprove of the intransitive use of the verb meaning "to have an effect": in our 2015 survey, 78 percent of the Panel (down only slightly from 85 percent in 2001) rejected *These policies are impacting on our ability to achieve success.* The transitive version was once as vilified, but is gradually becoming more acceptable: in 2015, only 50 percent (down from 80 percent in 2001) rejected *The court ruling will impact the education of minority students,* and only 39 percent (down from 66 percent in 2001) found the literal sense unacceptable in the sentence *Thousands of meteors have impacted the lunar surface.* Although resistance to the transitive senses is waning, the intransitive use is still strongly disliked and is best avoided.

4.3 Syntactic structure

How words are arranged in a sentence (or, put simply, syntax) is one of the more stable aspects of English.

One way to analyze sentences is to view them as a combination of a subject and a predicate. The subject is anchored by a noun, and the predicate is anchored by a verb. The subject consists of a noun or noun phrase, which itself may consist of other phrases, and the predicate consists of a verb or verb phrase, which itself may consist of other phrases.

- Statements (also called DECLARATIVE SENTENCES) generally begin with the subject, followed by the verb and the object. In the simple sentence *Delores ate an apple*, "Delores" is the subject, "ate" is the verb, and "an apple" is the object of the verb.
- Commands (also called IMPERATIVE SENTENCES) often omit the subject: *Eat an apple!*
- Questions (also called INTERROGATIVE SENTENCES) generally begin with the verb, or with a WH– WORD (the adverbs *who, what, where, when, why, how*) followed by a verb: *Did Delores eat an apple? What did Delores eat?*

If you're familiar with early Modern English works, like Shakespeare's plays or the King James Bible, you might know that questions were sometimes formed without using "do" or "did." For example, in *Troilus and Cressida*, Cressida says "And whither go they?" (That is, "Where do they go?" or "Where are they going?") Although this construction sounds odd to our modern ears, it was more common several centuries ago. (This is still the regular question structure in languages like German: *Und wohin gehen sie?*) The increased use of *do* when asking questions in place of inverting the subject and the verb is a simple example of how English has changed over time.

Something you can do!

The content of books from the 1600s and 1700s is easily found on the internet. You can access such texts at books.google. com, www.gutenberg.org, or archive.org or conduct a search on phrases like "books in the public domain." You can also access concordances of authors from that period at websites like opensourceshakespeare.org.

- Find three examples of English sentences from the 1600s or 1700s with an unusual sentence structure.
- Analyze how the sentences constructions are different from how they would be written in today's English.
- Rewrite the sentence in current English.

4.3.1 Rules of syntax versus rules of grammar

The rules of syntax are different from the rules of grammar. You're often taught specific "grammar rules" in school – but often these have more to do with style than grammar (a subject we will return to in Chapter 8). These PRESCRIPTIVE grammar rules are arbitrary, and how much they are considered to represent "proper" or "correct" English varies. A DESCRIPTIVE approach *describes* how people actually use language. A prescriptive approach *prescribes* – that is, sets down or establishes – rules for people to follow when using language.

Here are examples of prescriptive grammar rules:

- "Don't split an infinitive." (Use *to go boldly* instead of *to boldly go*.)
- "Don't end a sentence with a preposition." (Use *To whom did you give the ball?* and not *Who did you give the ball to?*)
- "Use subject pronouns in the subject position." (Use *Tom and I went to the park* and not *Me and Tom went to the park*.

These kinds of rules are commonly taught in school. Many issues of style are taught because they are not learned naturally like the way you learned that determiners (like *the*) come before nouns (like *book*) and not after.

Many of these "incorrect" forms are ones that grammarians decided decades or centuries ago would be incorrect. Whether or not you follow a given rule varies on several factors – you might commonly use some or all of these above "incorrect" forms in casual speech but not in formal writing.

Something you can do!

- Study the following sentences:

    - I wanted to really go the beach./I wanted really to go to the beach.
    - Who did you buy this book from?/From whom did you buy this book?
    - Me and Kara went to class./Kara and I went to class.

- For each pair, in what situations would you use the first example? In what situations would you use the second example? Consider situations that involve speech and other situations that involve writing. Are there any examples you would never use? Why?
- For each pair, analyze the way you think the following people would judge you for using each form:

- your best friend
- your parent or caregiver
- your teacher
- your employer

Rules of syntax are not like the kinds of rules that have to be taught. Instead, the syntax of a language involves the sentence patterns that native speakers of a language learn as infants and young children and do not have to be taught. If you speak English as a native language, it is highly unlikely that anyone taught you that typically adjectives come before nouns: *a blue house, a wide street, a happy boy.* Similarly, if you speak Spanish as a native language, it is highly unlikely that anyone taught you that typically adjectives come after nouns: *una casa azul, una calle ancha, un niño feliz.*

No native speaker of English ever had to be taught that *mat cat the the on sat* is an ungrammatical sentence. If you're a native speaker of English, you know that *Who did you see Mary with?* is completely understandable and *Who did you see Mary and?* is not.

These rules that native speakers instinctively understand are the rules that constitute its syntax. (Informally, syntax is sometimes used to refer the "don't split an infinitive" kind of rule, but doing so muddies the distinction between *syntax* and *grammar*.)

4.3.2 Theories of syntactic structures

Since the 1950s, the ways linguists have analyzed sentence structure have varied from theory to theory. However, most of these theoretical frameworks share, or were originally based on, this common concept: representing sentence structure as a tree with branching nodes.

Few teachers instruct students how to diagram sentences nowadays. Perhaps you've heard your parents speak of it or have seen references to it in older books and movies. The process of diagramming a sentence involves analyzing each word by its part of speech and creating a visual representation of that sentence.[4] For example, Figure 4.1 is a diagram of the sentence *The clown gave a red balloon to each child*.

Sentence diagraming is a useful tool in teaching students sentence structure, but it doesn't capture the relationships between the words and phrases of a sentence. These relationships can be visually represented by using syntax trees. The exact form of a syntax tree varies from theory to theory, but one generic syntax tree structure for this sentence is shown in Figure 4.2. Instead of placing dots over the node where branching lines meet, different theories assign different labels

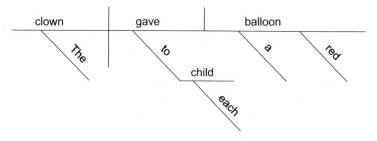

Figure 4.1 A sentence diagram.

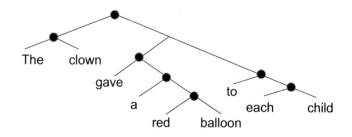

The clown gave a red balloon to each child.

Figure 4.2 A syntax tree.

to these points depending on each theory's categorization of the syntactic role assigned to each particular node.

Throughout the 1960s and 1970s, syntacticians concerned themselves with DEEP STRUCTURE, the underlying form of sentences upon which a series of transformations is performed to create more complex sentences. A statement like *Kyle drove to the store* undergoes a sequence of transformations to yield the question *Did Kyle drive to the store?* The use of *do, does*, and *did* to form questions is called DO SUPPORT. In these theories, a do-support transformation changes the underlying structure of *Kyle drove to the store* into *Kyle did drive to the store*. Then, an inversion transformation yields *Did Kyle drive to the store?* (Other transformations have the effect of emphasizing certain parts of the sentence, resulting in sentences like *Where Kyle drove was the store* or *It was Kyle who drove to the store.*)

Each language has its own deep structures. Each deep structure undergoes transformations that result in a specific syntactic manifestation of that sentence, called the SURFACE STRUCTURE. Then, a language-specific phonological component is laid onto the surface structure to yield the phonological realization of that sentence.

Since the 1960s, the primary theory of syntax has dealt with the syntactic framework as developed and promulgated by the US linguist Noam Chomsky. Chomsky's view of syntax is based on the biological basis by which humans are able to learn language. In the beginning of his career, his focus was examining the relationship between deep structures and how this manifested itself in spoken language in surface structure. The academic studies of that time put a lot of focus on the transformations that occurred when sentences were generated from the underlying deep structure.

Later, in order to encompass a greater variety of data from languages worldwide, this focus on specific transformations became more abstract. Over the course of decades, Chomsky's work shifted from looking at specific manifestations of how language was represented to studying the underpinnings of the biological component of grammar.[5] Some syntacticians focus on universal elements of syntax that arise from a biological language component. Others focus on the syntactic patterns of specific languages.[6]

When linguists hypothesize about language itself, they must take into account the linguistic diversity of thousands of living (and dead) languages. It's impossible to make statements about language itself by only focusing on a handful of languages from the same language family. This underscores the need to study and analyze languages from across the globe, especially endangered ones. In section 7.5, we'll see how making assumptions about how language works based on one's knowledge of one's own language can cloud linguistic judgments when analyzing languages from other language families.

4.3.3 Changes in syntax over time

Unlike phonetic systems, which can shift within decades, the syntactic structure of a language remains relatively stable. Nonetheless, change does occur.

In Chapter 1, we discussed the beginning of the epic poem *Beowulf*. As stated, Old English had a much more robust case system than Modern English does. Pronouns, for example, had dative and accusative forms, which merged into one form (often now referred to as the OBLIQUE CASE). For example, the same word, *her*, is used both as a direct object (*I saw her*) and as an indirect object (*I gave her the book*). In Old English, these forms would have been represented by the accusative and the dative cases, respectively.

Similarly, Old English employed sentence structures that have since dropped out of the language. In Modern English, the subject of a sentence is normally expressed with the nominative case. You say *I am cold* or *I like the book* – the word *I* is in the nominative case. In contrast, the literal German translation of *I am cold* is *Ich bin kalt*. However, *Ich bin kalt* doesn't refer to the speaker being cold in temperature but rather cold in personality. To express coldness in temperature, you would say *Mir ist kalt* – literally "To me is cold." This construction also occurs in many Slavic languages. In Czech, you would say *Je mi zima* – literally "It is to me cold." The German pronoun *mir* and the Czech pronoun *mi* are dative forms of the first person singular; this construction is known as a DATIVE CONSTRUCTION.

These constructions were more common in Old English, became less common in Middle English, and became almost nonexistent in Modern English. Examples that are still somewhat familiar to Modern English speakers include *methinks* and *meseems*, which both mean "it seems to me." Here is an example from Shakespeare's *Hamlet*: *The lady doth protest too much, methinks.*

Another way that English syntax has changed over time has to do with word order. English is known as an SVO LANGUAGE. In an SVO language, declarative sentences typically follow a subject-verb-object word order. That is, the subject is followed by the verb, which is followed by the object:

> *The apple fell to the ground.*
> *She ate a strawberry.*
> *I bought a new bicycle.*

Of course, other orders are found in English. Verbs and subjects are transposed in questions, for example. Or you can place emphasis through word order. *It was a bicycle I bought* places emphasis on the object being bought – in this case a bicycle, as opposed to a car, book, or diamond ring. As a default, however, Modern English follows the subject-verb-object pattern.

Old English, however, is considered an SOV LANGUAGE. In an SOV language, declarative sentences typically follow a subject-object-verb word order. Whether the change occurred abruptly when Old English transitioned into Middle English or more gradually is a topic of academic debate. Regardless of whether the change was swift or gradual, the typical word order of Old English is different than those of Middle and Modern English.

4.3.4 Syntactic variation

English syntactic variation is relatively limited in comparison to phonetic variation. Examples include:

- *need + Xed verbal constructions*: Typically, you would say sentences like *The car needs to be washed* or *The rug needs to be vacuumed.* But especially in Pittsburgh, southwestern Pennsylvania, and nearby areas of Ohio and West Virginia, you're likely to hear *The car needs washed* or *The rug needs vacuumed.* Many linguists attribute this construction to Scots-Irish influence.

- *a-Xing verb constructions*: In some rural areas of the southern United States, you might hear sentences like *He was a-running* (often with alveolar [n] instead of velar [ŋ] – that is, *He was a-runnin'*), with verbs stressed on the first syllable. The *American Heritage Dictionary* states that the *a* derives from the Old English preposition *on*, which was used in a similar construction to indicate ongoing action.

- *Give it me*: The phrasing *Give it me* (for *Give it to me*) is a feature of varieties spoken in northern England. A map at the "Our Dialects" project of the University of Manchester (projects.alc. manchester.ac.uk/ukdialectmaps/syntactic-variation/give-it-me/) shows that respondents from northern England accept this construction more than other parts of the United Kingdom.

- *double modals* (also called *multiple modals*): One feature of varieties spoken in the southern United States, African American English, northern England, and Scotland is the occurrence of double modals, like *She **might could** know the answer.* This construction contrasts with typical sentences like *She might know the answer* or *She could know the answer.*[7]

4.4 Conclusion

In this chapter, we've looked at the structure of sentences, phrases, and clauses. We discussed the parts of speech and how words are ordered in sentences. We've compared the rules of grammar to the rules of syntax and examined syntactic variation.[8] In the next chapter, we'll look at the philosophical concept of meaning and how words convey meaning.

4.5 Questions for discussion

- How are phrases, clauses, and sentences similar? How are they different?

- What are the parts of speech? Give some examples of each.
- How would you describe the difference between grammar and syntax? Give some examples of each.
- In certain situations, do you break or bend some rules of grammar? If so, why?
- Why do you think the syntax of a language changes more slowly than phonetic features?

Notes

1 Further Reading: The *American Heritage Student Grammar Dictionary* provides clear and simple explanations of grammar terms, including those found in this chapter.
2 You can view the *Schoolhouse Rock* video "Interjections!" (lyrics by Lynn Ahrens) at http://video.disney.com/watch/interjections-school-house-rock-disney-shorts-502a710d36516abe09ecf58b
3 Bill Waterson, "Calvin and Hobbes" strip (January 25, 1993), *Go Comics*, www.gocomics.com/calvinandhobbes/1993/01/25
4 Further Reading: You can find more about sentence diagramming on Lisa McLendon's blog, *Madam Grammar* (online access at https://madam grammar.com/category/diagramming/).
5 Further Reading: John Collins, *Chomsky: A Guide for the Perplexed*. This book details the evolution of Chomsky's theories.
6 Further Reading: James McCawley, *The Syntactic Phenomena of English*, volumes 1 and 2. These books describe English syntactic patterns.
7 Further Reading: The Yale Grammatical Diversity Project article "Multiple Modals" (online access at https://ygdp.yale.edu/phenomena/multiple-modals).
8 Further Reading: Maggie Tallerman, *Understanding Syntax*.

Chapter 5

Word meaning

5.0 Introduction

In earlier chapters, we examined how you can combine sounds to form syllables and words, and how you can combine words to form phrases, clauses, and sentences.

Through words, humans are able to convey thoughts, feelings, and more to others.

In this chapter, we will examine these topics:

- how dictionaries and other authoritative reference works account for including the subset of possible words of a language that they do
- how lexicographers define words
- how the meanings of English words change over time and how new meanings arise
- how the meanings of English words vary from geographical region to region
- how philosophers and linguists have analyzed meaning

The study of meaning is called SEMANTICS. The study of word meaning is called LEXICAL SEMANTICS.

When a person transmits information to other people by using language, the people being addressed are the AUDIENCE. An audience can consist of one person or of more than one person. Kinds of audiences include:

- people who hear something communicated in spoken language

- people who apprehend something communicated in sign language
- people who read something communicated in written language

(Some theorists use other terms for *audience*, including ADDRESSEES and UNDERSTANDERS. Still other terms, like OVERHEARERS and LISTENERS, apply only to spoken language. For some, an *audience* refers to anyone who hears, sees, or reads the communication; for others, an *audience* only includes people who understand the language being spoken, signed, or written in. When *audience* is used in this book, it's from the point of view that the communicator intends to be understood.)

How do you communicate thoughts to an audience? You might communicate by uttering a string of phonetic sounds, making signs in a manual language, or writing a series of characters. Meaningful units of these sounds, signs, or written characters are often what we would consider to be words. With these words, we convey our thoughts to others.

5.1 Words, reference works, and authority

Communication is successful if one person is able to convey a message to another person. Some people look to authoritative reference works like dictionaries and style guides as arbiters of how to best communicate. (Of course, reference works aren't limited to dictionaries and style guides: atlases, etiquette books, manuals, concordances, lists of laws going back to the Code of Hammurabi – humanity has for millennia referred to such collections for information.[1])

Most major languages have dictionaries that list the words of the language and describe what those words mean. Some countries have a governing body that decides which words are acceptable in the official language of that country. For example, the official language of France is French. In France, an institution called the *Académie française* determines whether a word is considered French or not. (Of course, other languages besides French are spoken in France. We will discuss minority languages in France in section 7.2.3.)

There is no equivalent of the *Académie française* for English in the United States or in the United Kingdom. Dictionaries are published by many companies in both countries, as well as in Canada, India,

Australia, and other countries where English is an official language. However, none of these dictionaries is the final arbiter of what is officially considered to be an English word and what is not.

For centuries, people have obsessed over what is and is not a word. Is *ain't* a word? (Yes, it is!) In the 1960s, *Webster's Third New International Dictionary*, published by Merriam-Webster, became the focus of widespread criticism because the editorial staff chose to enter the word *ain't*. Despite this criticism, most other American dictionaries soon included *ain't* as well, including *The American Heritage Dictionary of the English Language*, which had originally been conceived to combat the "permissiveness" that *Webster's Third* was thought to have. (David Skinner's *The Story of Ain't* chronicles how *ain't* came to be included in *Webster's Third* and the subsequent public response.)

But a word does not have to be enshrined in a dictionary to actually be a word! No one Modern English dictionary accounts for every word that is or can be used: the English language changes too quickly and is too vast to be completely cataloged.

Further, English is very productive. A PRODUCTIVE rule is a pattern that allows you to form other words that follow that pattern. The present participle of verbs is formed by adding the productive morpheme *–ing*. When a new verb enters the lexicon, you know that its present participle is formed by adding *–ing*, like *eat/eating*.) You can add a productive prefix like *pre–* to almost any verb to indicate that the action is being undertaken ahead of the customary time. You can add the productive prefix *non–* to almost any adjective to indicate the opposite of that adjective. Many dictionaries list hundreds of *pre–* and *non–* words, but no dictionary lists all of them.

Only dictionaries of dead languages can account for every word in those languages. Tocharian B was an Indo-European language spoken in an area of what is now northwestern China. Archaeologists have uncovered examples of Tocharian B that were written roughly between the fifth to ninth centuries CE. So, a dictionary of Tocharian B can list every word that is known to exist in Tocharian B.

The *Middle English Dictionary* – which you can access at quod.lib. umich.edu/m/med – lists all Middle English words that exist in known texts from that period. But there's no way of knowing about Middle

English words that existed but that were never written down in known Middle English documents.

Originally, the physical limitations of printed publications meant that dictionary editors couldn't include all the content that they would have liked to. Once dictionary content could be presented in an electronic format, space concerns stopped being an issue. The amount of material in an electronic dictionary is limited only by the amount of content its editors can compile. But even though an online dictionary is not restricted in size, there is still no one source that contains every possible English word.

Free from the physical restrictions of printed books, all kinds of dictionaries can be found on the internet. There are general dictionaries that define the lexicon of a single language. There are multilingual dictionaries that provide translations across languages. There are specialized dictionaries that cover terminology in specific fields like medicine or law. There are crowdsourced dictionaries compiled by online contributors, such as Urban Dictionary. Even reference works that are not curated by a professional staff are useful resources because they provide evidence for the way people use language.

5.2 Defining words

Writing a dictionary entry is harder than you might initially think!

Something you can do!

- Try defining the following words: *red, table, in, walk.*
- Compare your definition with those found in a curated dictionary like the *Oxford English Dictionary* (oed. com),[2] the *Merriam-Webster's Collegiate Dictionary* (merriam-webster.com), or the *American Heritage Dictionary* (ahdictionary.com).
- How many senses were you able to account for? What was difficult about wording the senses?
- Compile a list of four to five newer words that aren't included in those dictionaries and define those terms. Compare your definitions with those that you find in an

> online dictionary like Urban Dictionary. How similar or
> different are they?

Drafting a dictionary entry is a time-consuming, complicated process. An editor who researches, writes, and edits the definitions found in dictionaries is called a LEXICOGRAPHER. When considering whether a word should be included in a dictionary, lexicographers examine CITATIONS – examples of the use of the word in question.

In years past, editors or volunteer readers would read books, magazines, and newspapers, seeking out examples of usages of words. The sentence, paragraph, or phrase was copied, or cut out and pasted, onto a small notecard. Editors sorted these cards into piles based on how the word was used. Nowadays, this work is largely conducted electronically by analyzing information in a CORPUS. A corpus is a vast collection of written and spoken language. (The plural of *corpus* is *corpora*.) Modern corpora often have hundreds of millions of words; some are approaching or have reached one billion words.

In comparing and contrasting the ways word is used, its meanings are teased apart.

When defining a noun, the first step is determining the category that the word is a member of: *uranium* is "an element." A *dog* is "an animal," "a mammal," or "a vertebrate mammal," depending on the complexity of the dictionary. This word that describes the entry word (*element, animal*, and *mammal*) is called the GENUS of the definition. What follows the genus is information that separates one word from others sharing the same genus: while a *pen* and a *pencil* are both writing implements, the former contains ink and the latter graphite.

Something you can do!

* Compare five words in the same category – for example, choose five mammals (cat, dog, horse, pig, fox), five colors (red, orange, blue, green, yellow), or five sports (baseball, basketball, soccer, hockey, football).

- Based on your own experience, describe how the five items in the category you've chosen are different. (That is, if your category was *colors*, consider how is *red* different from *orange* and *blue*, and so forth.)
- Compare your descriptions with definitions from a dictionary. What parts of your definition were the same as ones in the dictionary? What information does the dictionary provide that you did not? What information did you provide that the dictionary did not?

If you're interested in learning more about how words are added to dictionaries, read Kory Stamper's *Word by Word*. (Stamper also has a blog, *Harmless Drudgery*, at korystamper.wordpress.com about "defining the words that define us.") For a scholarly approach to dictionary development, including the structure of entries, refer to Sidney Landau's *Dictionaries: The Art and Craft of Lexicography*. For a historical look at the development of the *Oxford English Dictionary*, read Simon Winchester's *The Professor and the Madman*. Although it's fiction, the Japanese novel *The Great Passage* by Shion Miura (which has also been made into a movie and a manga series) vividly describes the process of creating a dictionary.

Chapter 8 discusses usage information found in dictionaries and style guides.

5.3 Changes in the meaning of words

Of all the types of language change discussed in this book, the examples that come to your mind most easily probably involve words. Changes in pronunciation occur within a speech community very slowly. The Northern Cities Shift that we looked at in section 2.6 spread slowly away from urban centers, mostly along interstate expressway routes, over the course of several decades. Changes in sentence structure take even more time to spread throughout a population. Most people never witness abrupt syntactic change during of their lifetime.

5.3.1 Change over time

The meanings of words can and do change rapidly. You encounter new senses of existing words all the time. This doesn't refer to learning new vocabulary words (like *effulgent* or *voracious*) that have been in the language for a long time. Rather, you often encounter new meanings that didn't previously exist.

Words can acquire new senses. When new technologies are developed, many words that refer to these technological advances already exist. Even though brand-new words may be coined, often an existing word acquires a new meaning. *Scroll, cut, paste, pinch,* and *swipe* are all very old verbs in English. In recent decades, these verbs have acquired new meanings to describe functions used with computers, cell phones, touchscreens, and other electronic technology.

JARGON is the terminology used in a particular occupation. In journalism, *dek, hed*, and *lede* describe different parts of an article and are differentiated from *deck, head*, and *lead*. *Lede* (the first sentence or introduction of a news story) is useful because *lead* has many meanings and two pronunciations. As the internet's 24/7 news cycle has made journalism more transparent to laypeople, these words are now more familiar to the general population.

Scientific and medical terminology changes very rapidly as new discoveries are made. The slang used by social groups, such as teenagers, changes rapidly and varies from group to group.

Something you can do!

- Find three words that have acquired new meanings since the time you were born.
- Find three words that didn't exist before you were born. (You can use an online dictionary to help you with these tasks.)
- Discuss these terms with your classmates. Do these words fall into any particular categories? How many of these words would you say are slang terms?

The way words are used changes over time. For example, you might be surprised to learn that use of *impact* and *contact* as verbs was once greatly frowned upon. (Section 8.2.5 details how attitudes about *contact* have changed since the 1960s.) Often when nouns start to be used as verbs, or when verbs start to be used as nouns, there's a period of resistance. That resistance over the years often fades away.

Change can result from an attempt to sound original or current. A term is introduced in the popular culture – through movies, television, or song, and fans begin to use it. (Sometimes this process is mocked, as in the oft-quoted line from the movie *Mean Girls*: "Gretchen, stop trying to make *fetch* happen!") Often older generations are turned off by change – elders and "protectors of language" have been complaining about the youth of society ruining the language for millennia. Modern condemnation that the use of emojis or texting is ruining the language is analogous to condemnation by people who worried language was going to be ruined by telegraph communication, by comic books, by television, by the internet, and so forth. Sociological factors of language change will be explored further in Chapter 7.

Here are examples of how words change over time:

5.3.1.1 Social changes

In the late 1800s and early 1900s, categorization was an important scientific tool. This tendency to categorize can be seen in the detailed way the United States census categorized people by race, using specialized terminology (*mulatto*, *quadroon*) for people whose parents or grandparents belonged to different racial categories.

Moron, imbecile, and *idiot* were all originally part of a classification system that indicated different degrees of intellectual disability. (*Intellectual disability* is itself a phrase that the medical community has recently begun using instead of the phrase *mental retardation.*) Over time, *moron, imbecile*, and *idiot* came to be used more generically as an insult.

5.3.1.2 Legal changes

Marriage provides a good example of how the definition of a word can change. In many parts of the United States, marriage was illegal between people of different races until the Supreme Court in *Loving v. Virginia* ruled that laws banning interracial marriage were unconstitutional. Marriage was restricted to two people of the opposite sex until countries (beginning with the Netherlands in 2001), provinces of Canada (beginning with Ontario in 2003), and states of the US (beginning with Massachusetts in 2004), allowed marriage between people of the same sex. As more jurisdictions adopted legislation that allowed same-sex couples to marry, the definition of *marriage* changed. That, in turn, required redefining words like *husband, aunt,* and *widower* to allow for same-sex couples.[3]

5.3.1.3 Scientific changes

As new scientific discoveries and advances are made, words are either created or existing words are revised. New chemical elements are named (*darmstadtium, roenteginum, tennessine*) as they are synthesized. As mentioned, advances in technology often use existing terminology in an extended sense – scrolling was once something you did with physical scrolls, and now it is an action you can execute on documents that you're viewing onscreen. Virtually every scientific field is a fertile ground for the development of new words:

- astronomy (*cubewano, exoplanet, magnetar*)
- genetics (*exome, genomics, homeobox*)
- quantum physics (*nanocrystal, oscillon, qubit*)

5.3.2 Changes across locations

Change is noticeable in different ways: the changes you see over time in a given area, and the changes you see at one time across different areas. It is easy to see differences in words in English, because the meanings of words can vary from region to region, and the words that are used to convey different meanings can change from region to region.

Due to England's history as a colonial power, the English language spread across the globe centuries ago. English is the official language or an official language in many countries outside of the United Kingdom, including Canada, the United States, South Africa, India,

Australia, and New Zealand. Oxford University Press, the publisher of the *Oxford English Dictionary*, has dictionaries specific to English as it is spoken in many of these countries. Many dictionaries explore the varieties of English in these places. Among the first was Henry Yule's *Hobson-Jobson*, a glossary first published in 1886 that defines and explains words brought into English from languages spoken on the Indian subcontinent in the 1800s.[4]

You might be familiar with word differences between the United States and the United Kingdom. Here is a small list:

United States	United Kingdom
hood/trunk (of a car)	bonnet/boot
vacation	holiday
pharmacist	chemist
lift	elevator

And, the same word can have different meanings. For example, *football* in the United States is different from *football* in England. What the English call *football*, Americans call *soccer*.

Lynne Murphy is an American linguist who is a professor in England, where she has lived since 2000. Her blog *Separated by a Common Language* and her book *The Prodigal Tongue* are great resources for distinctions between British and American English.

Something you can do!

- Think of a distinction between British English and American English and search on Murphy's blog (separatedbyacommon language.blogspot.com) to see if she has discussed this topic.
- Prepare a short description of three topics that she has addressed in her blogs. (At the drop-down menu, search on the 'topic' labels.)
- Share these descriptions with your class.

Some concepts are expressed by the same words in the United States and the United Kingdom but are expressed differently in other countries where English is spoken. For example, in the United States and the United Kingdom, 1,000 is a thousand, 1,000,000 is a million, and 1,000,000,000 is a billion.[5] These large numbers are grouped in chunks of three digits.

On the Indian subcontinent, however, numbers are broken down differently. One *lakh* is equal to one hundred thousand (100,000) and is written as 1,00,000. One hundred lakh is a *crore*, equal to ten million (10,000,000) and is written as 1,00,00,000. In the English of the Indian subcontinent, above a thousand, numbers are grouped in chunks of two digits.

What's referred to by the plant called *corn* varies regionally. Often *corn* refers to the primary grain that is grown in a particular region. In the United States, *corn* is what other English-speaking countries call *maize*. In Scotland, *corn* is what North Americans would refer to as *oats*. In England, *corn* either refers to grain in general, or specifically to wheat. *Corn* in the general sense of "a grain" or "a seed" is also found in words like *barleycorn* and *peppercorn*.

Here are examples of vocabulary from other countries where English is the official language or one of the official languages:

- *Australia:* A *bikkie* is a biscuit. This refers to the British English sense of *biscuit*, and is what would be referred to as a *cookie* in the United States.
- *Canada*: A *parkade* is a parking garage with two or more levels.
- *Hong Kong*: A *godown* is a warehouse. (This word comes from Malay, an Austronesian language of Malaysia, the Malay Peninsula, and nearby areas.)
- *New Zealand*: A *Pakeha* is a New Zealander whose ancestry is European, in contrast to the indigenous Maori population. (This word comes from Maori, an Austronesian language of New Zealand.)
- *South Africa*: A *kloof* is a deep ravine. (This word comes from Afrikaans, a Germanic language that developed from the Dutch spoken by early colonialists.)

You don't have to travel internationally to compare differences in English vocabulary. Meaning varies within national borders as well. Carbonated beverages are referred to by many words in different regions of the United States, including *soda, pop, soft drink*, and *tonic*. In the United Kingdom, there are many words for *alleyway*, including *snicket, ginnel*, and *chare*.[6] (We'll explore regional variation further in section 7.4.)

5.4 Meaning and usage

Language is adaptable. If a person is able to convey what they mean to another person, communication is successful. Although Chapter 8 is dedicated to the topics of rules, usage, and style, it's worth pointing out in our discussion of meaning how failure to distinguish between words can lead to communication failure. A good example of a style guideline that has to do with meaning involves the word *inflammable*, which happens to mean the same thing as *flammable*. If you're using *inflammable* to mean *nonflammable*, you are not going to be able to effectively communicate with people who are aware of the distinction. You're of course free to say what you want, but if you're in charge of making sure people don't get burned, you'll want to be sure that communication is successful.

Sometimes resistance to some words is so strong that it is unlikely the stigma associated with such words will be lifted. In section 5.1 we discussed *ain't*. Another example of a highly stigmatized word is *irregardless*. Likely you have heard the claim that *irregardless* is not a word, despite how common it actually is. Opponents claim that the negative prefix *ir–* is redundant with the negative suffix *–less*. (However, *debone* means the same thing as *bone*; *unravel* means the same thing as *ravel* – and no one complains about the redundancy in these words). Resistance to *irregardless* is a tradition – it's been that way for decades, and eventual acceptance is unlikely because it is a poster child for "words that aren't words." Really, though, it's an example of the arbitrariness of stylistic rules of a language.[7]

Something you can do!

Research the distinction in meaning of the following sets of words. Check at least three different reference works.

* *flaunt* and *flout*
* *reluctant* and *reticent*
* *enormousness* and *enormity*
* *imply* and *infer*
* *persuade* and *convince*

In your opinion, is the distinction necessary to prevent confusion? Or, is the distinction a pedantic style issue that really doesn't matter?

We will return to these questions of style in Chapter 8.

5.5 Academic approaches to meaning

There are many linguistic approaches to analyzing meaning. Some theorists proposed breaking down words into a collection of binary oppositions: *girl* could be seen as being composed of the elements +human | +female (or –male) | +child (or –adult). Although many English words can be analyzed like this, far more words (like *inequality* or *cement* or *myopia*) don't lend themselves to this analysis.

Other linguists have attempted to describe language in completely logical terms using functions (called OPERATORS) like *if*, *then*, and *it is true that*. (This framework is called PREDICATE LOGIC.) Such approaches narrow "meaning" down to the conditions under which sentences can be true or false.

A sentence does not have to be true to have meaning. The sentence *It is raining outside* reports on a meteorological condition at or near the person making that statement. It can be categorized as true or false. If it is, in fact, raining outside, this sentence is true. If it is not raining outside, this sentence is false.

Here's another statement: *Montreal is the capital of Canada.* What about that? Montreal is *not* the capital of Canada; Ottawa is. Yet, we understand the meaning of that sentence, and we know that in the world we live in, this sentence is false. (You can imagine a parallel universe to ours where the only difference is the capital of Canada in that world is Montreal; for that world, this statement would be true.) In other words, false statements have meaning.

As an introductory overview to academic approaches to meaning, we'll look at the work of four important scholars.

5.5.1 Ferdinand de Saussure (1857–1913)

Ferdinand de Saussure, a Swiss linguist and philosopher, was one of the early scholars who formulated and influenced the development of semantics as an academic study. His book *Course in General Linguistics* was published in 1916 by his students after his death. This book lays the groundwork for most semantic theories of the 20th century. Although Saussure wrote in French and used Latin examples, for simplicity, English equivalents will be used in this discussion. (Quoted material in this section is from a 1983 translation by Roy Harris.)

Before Saussure, philosophers who studied meaning contended mostly with the historical development of a word or comparison of words and word forms among languages. Saussure was among the first philosophers to analyze the distinction between *langue* and *parole*. Although these French words are usually translated into English with *language* and *speech*, Saussure meant more by these terms. He used *langue* to refer to a collection of SIGNS (as opposed to words) understood by a sociocultural group (like all the users of a language). *Parole* refers to the actual instances of the use of *langue*, including both speech and writing, by everyone who uses it.

Saussure posited that the linguistic sign *tree* is the union of the concept of a tree and the sensory impression that is formed by a specific instance of uttering or writing this word. He calls the "concept" the SIGNIFIED and the "sensory impression" the SIGNIFIER and says these two elements are "both psychological and are connected in the brain by an associative link." Each sign exists in the mind as a two-sided entity; awareness of one side triggers awareness of the other.

Importantly, the link between these two elements, and therefore the sign itself, is *arbitrary*. (This is easily proven given the existence of different words in different languages: what is called a *tree* in English is called *arbol* in Spanish, *arbor* in French, and so forth.) It's not arbitrary in the sense that a person can't use whatever term they want (if you used *spoon*, *splurbo*, or *bzzzzt!* for "tree," you would not be understood), but rather that there is "no natural connection in reality": there is no reason why the utterance of the phonemes [t] [r] [i] in sequence means *tree* – it's an arbitrary fact of English that they do.

One of the most important contributions of Saussure to linguistics was the recognition that in order to understand reality, you needed to understand "the social use of verbal signs."

5.5.2 Zeno Vendler (1921–2004)

The way words are categorized semantically tells you things about how they can be used in sentences. It's not enough to know that a given word is, say, a noun or a verb. If a word is a verb, what kind of noun phrases relate to it? If a word is a noun, what kind of roles can that noun play with respect to different verbs? In analyzing these interactions, patterns emerge.

Zeno Vendler, an American philosopher who taught in Canada, published an article in 1957 called *Verbs and Times*. He categorized verbs based on whether they describe whether events exist, pass, or come to completion over a period of time.

As you recall from section 4.2.2, verbs can be *intransitive* – ones that don't take an object, like *sleep* (*I slept soundly*) – or *transitive* – ones that take objects, like *cut* (*I cut the paper*). The kinds of words and phrases that occur with verbs aren't arbitrary. The sentence **I slept the paper* makes no sense. (The asterisk indicates that a sentence is not well-formed according to the rules of a language.)

Vendler analyzed how some verbs (like *run*) are more likely to be used in the progressive aspect (the aspect of a verb that expresses an ongoing action) and how some aren't (like *know*). *I am running* makes sense in a way that *I am knowing* doesn't. In response to a question like *What are you doing?*, *I am running* is a possible answer, whereas *I am knowing* is not. Words like *running* and *writing* are "processes in time." That is, they can be broken into processes that follow each other in sequence. Words like *knowing* and *loving* do not describe processes in time. If you know how to speak French, you can't break down the process of your knowing the way you can describe the ordered sequence of physical movements of a person who is running.

Vendler observed what distinguishes verbs that are used in the progressive. He contrasted the sentences *I am running* and *I am drawing*, with *I am running a mile* and *I am drawing a circle.* In the first two examples, the duration of the activity is not implied. If you are running, and you stop, you can say that you ran. If you are running a mile, and you stop before you reach the mile, you cannot say you ran a mile. He refers to verbs used in sentences like *I am running* as ACTIVITY TERMS and verbs in sentences like *I am running a mile* as ACCOMPLISHMENT TERMS. (Note that a verb, like *run*, can be either an activity term or an accomplishment term, depending on its use.)

Something you can do!

- Create two sentences for each of these words: *write, sing, eat, sew.* In one sentence, use an activity term. For the other, use an accomplishment term. (Using *draw* as an example, a sentence associated with the activity term could be *I am drawing*, and with the accomplishment term *I am drawing a circle*.)

Vendler categorized verbs like *spot* and *believe* that don't naturally use the progressive in two ways: ACHIEVEMENT TERMS, which describe events that occur at a single moment, and STATE TERMS, for those which last for a period of time. *Spot* is an achievement term: *When did you spot the plane?* can be answered with a specific time: *at 10:00. Believe* is a state term: *When did you believe in Santa Claus?* can be answered with a duration: *until I was 7*. It is odd to say **I spotted the plane for three hours* or **I believed in Santa at 3:30*.

This article is an important part of the foundation for later research in this area.

5.5.3 Charles Fillmore (1929–2014)

Charles Fillmore, an American linguistics professor, published in 1968 "The Case for Case," an examination of the semantic roles of noun phrases that occur with verbs. (There is an ambiguity between Fillmore's use of *case* and its use as a category in declensions of nouns in languages like Latin as discussed in section 3.2.1.1. Many scholars came to use SEMANTIC ROLE to refer to what Fillmore here calls *case*.)

Fillmore examined why certain sentences could be rephrased in ways that other could not. This pairing is among his most famous examples: You can say *I broke the glass* or *I hit the glass*. However, while *The glass broke* is grammatical, **The glass hit* is not grammatical. (Again, the asterisk indicates this sentence is ungrammatical.)

What is it about *break* that allows this sort of alternation? What is it about *hit* that does not? In Fillmore's 1970 article "The Grammar of Hitting and Breaking," he analyzes the class of verbs that operate like *break* and the class that operates like *hit*.

"The Case for Case" also establishes the terminology for the roles nouns can play in a sentence. In *John broke the window with a hammer*, these are the roles:

> *John* is the AGENT (the entity undertaking the action)
> *window* is the PATIENT (the entity that is acted upon)
> *hammer* is the INSTRUMENT (the entity that is used to carry out the action)

This leads to his observation that you can say *John broke the window*, and you can say *A hammer broke the window*, but you cannot say **John and a hammer broke the window*. This is because you can't conjoin two noun phrases that have different roles (in this case, Agent and Instrument.)

5.5.4 Beth Levin (born 1955)

Many scholars have expanded Fillmore's framework. Beth Levin, an American linguistics professor, in 1993 published *Verb Class Alternations.* One underlying principle of Levin's work is that a verb's grammatical behavior is largely determined by its meaning. (The behavior of a verb refers to the interpretation of the nouns, noun phrases, and prepositional phrases that are used with it.) That is, the syntactic behavior of a verb is semantically determined.

Here's an example from Levin's introduction regarding *spray* and *load*. These two verbs act similarly. They can take two arguments, and those arguments can be expressed in two ways.

> 1a. Sharon sprayed the water on the plants.
> 1b. Sharon sprayed the plants with water.
> 2a. The farmer loaded apples into the cart.
> 2b. The farmer loaded the cart with apples.

The difference in expression between the (a) sentences and the (b) sentences is sometimes called the LOCATIVE ALTERNATION.

Something you can do!

- Analyze the verbs *cover, fill, pour*, and *dump*.
- Determine which of these verbs share the paradigm that *spray* and *load* do.

From this exercise, you see that *pour* and *dump* allow for the syntactic structure in 1a and 2a. *Fill* and *cover* allow for the syntactic structure in 1b and 2b. Here are more of Levin's examples:

> *Monica covered a blanket over the baby.
> Monica covered the baby with a blanket.

> *Gina filled lemonade into the pitcher.
> Gina filled the pitcher with lemonade.

*Carla poured the pitcher with lemonade.
Carla poured lemonade into the pitcher.

The farmer dumped apples into the car.
*The farmer dumped the cart with apples.

Native speakers of English acquire these patterns subconsciously and do not have to be taught them. People who learn English as a second language have to be taught these facts about these words. In knowing what a verb means, a speaker understands its behavior.

Levin states that verbs fall into classes based on "shared components of meaning." Regular relationships between meaning and behavior mean that a "verb's behavior arises from the interaction of its meaning and general principles of grammar." The connection between the grammatical behavior and the meaning of a verb is not specific to English. Analogous verb alternations are found across languages.

5.6 Conclusion

In this chapter, we examined how the meanings of words are defined in dictionaries and other reference works. We looked at the changes in the meaning of words over time and across locations. We looked at philosophy of meaning, how meaning is conveyed, and the semantic role of words in sentences.

What about sentences that express meaning indirectly? Why does *Can you shut the window?* function as a request to shut the window and not as a question of one's ability to shut a window? We tackle this topic in the next chapter.

5.7 Questions for discussion

- In France, the *Académie française* determines whether a word is considered French or not. There's no equivalent of this institution for English. How does that affect how people use English?
- Why do complete dictionaries only exist for dead languages?
- How does defining a noun differ from defining a verb?

- List some things that are called by different names in different English-speaking countries. List some things are called by different names within the United States or within the United Kingdom.
- Is *ain't* a word?
- Why is analyzing the kinds of nouns that can be used with specific verbs important?

Notes

1 Further Reading: Jack Lynch, *You Could Look It Up*. This is a reference book about reference books "from ancient Babylon to Wikipedia."
2 If your institution doesn't have a subscription to the *Oxford English Dictionary*, oxforddictionaries.com has other searchable dictionary databases maintained by Oxford University Press.
3 Further Reading: Kory Stamper, *Word by Word,* the chapter titled "Marriage"; Steve Kleinedler, "The Semantics of Marriage Equality" (online access at www.advocate.com/news/news-features/2009/11/24/semantics-marriage-equality).
4 Further Reading: Traci Nagle's review of *Hobson-Jobson: The Definitive Glossary of British India,* by Henry Yule and A.C. Burnell, selected edition.
5 1,000,000,000 was once called a *milliard* in the United Kingdom. The US billion was a thousand million and the UK billion was a million million, or a US trillion. Since 1974, the United Kingdom has officially used the same numbering system as in the United States, whereby above a million, each new term is a thousand times greater instead of a million times greater.
6 Further Reading: "Alleyways of Language: Regional Worlds for 'Alleyway'" on the Oxford Dictionaries blog (online access at http://blog.oxforddictionaries.com/2014/10/regional-words-alleyway/).
7 Further Reading: Kory Stamper, *Word by Word*, the chapter titled "Irregardless."

Chapter 6

Context

6.0 Introduction

We examined meaning in the last chapter. We discussed meaning as a general concept and how we convey what we mean to other people. We also discussed the meaning of individual words, and how words are strung together to create meaningful sentences that other people understand.

In this chapter, we will look at communicating ideas that aren't literally conveyed by the meaning of the words themselves, but that rely on factors outside of semantics, like context. We will examine these topics:

- reference and context
- the principles of conversation
- how to do things with words
- discourse analysis
- politeness

PRAGMATICS is the study of language in context, including what we communicate beyond the meaning of the words we use.

6.1 Reference and context

REFERENCE allows our audience to identify something specific.

I. You know what *I* means. But who does *I* refer to? When I use the word *I*, I am referring to me, Steve Kleinedler. When you use the word *I*, *I* refers to yourself. When the author Mary Roach uses the word *I*, *I* refers to Mary Roach.

In other words, the reference of *I* is entirely dependent on context – specifically, who is the person who is using the word *I*? Similarly, context is required to know the referents of adverbs of place and time like *here* and *now* and demonstrative adjectives like *this* and *that*. Words like these whose meaning is dependent on context are called INDEXICALS.

The ability to describe the relationship between what we say and what we are referring to has been an important topic in linguistics since the 1890s, when Gottlob Frege, a German philosopher, published "Über Sinn und Bedeutung" ("On Sense and Reference.") Although his philosophy and the subsequent arguments and criticisms of other philosophers are too advanced for this introductory text, there are a few important concepts having to do with reference that are helpful to know and easy to understand.[1]

ANAPHORA is the use of a pronoun to refer to the same person or thing expressed by a word or phrase (generally a noun or noun phrase). In the sentence *An older gentleman entered the restaurant, and the waiter offered him a menu.* The use of *him* to refer to *An older gentlemen* is an example of anaphora. The word or phrase that the pronoun refers to is called the ANTECEDENT. In this example, *an older gentleman* is the antecedent. If the pronoun is used first, like *him* in the sentence *Near him, John saw a snake*, this phenomenon is called CATAPHORA. (Some scholars use *anaphora* to refer to both situations.)

DEIXIS is the function of an indexical in the specifying of its context-dependent referent. (*Deixis*, and its adjective form *deictic*, ultimately come from the Greek word meaning "to show.") So, in the sentence *Inez passed Bill on the street, and Bill waved to her – deixis* refers to the context-dependent specification of "her" to the referent, Inez. (Indexicals are sometimes referred to as *deictic words*.) Anaphora is an example of deixis.

6.2 Mutual knowledge

A colleague of mine, Elaine Francis, is an associate professor in the Department of English and the Linguistics Program at Purdue

University. She reported hearing the following sentence on a National Public Radio (NPR) program:

Beyoncé leads the Grammy nominees with nine.

When I read the sentence the first time, I immediately understood what the speaker was trying to convey: that Beyoncé led the nominees with nine nominations.

Then, Francis asked of her linguist friends whether we thought the sentence was ill-formed, so I re-read the sentence. Paying closer attention, I realized that *nine* refers to "nine nominations." But, there was no prior mention of the word *nominations*. From a semantic standpoint, the sentence about Beyoncé would be considered ill-formed because *nine* has no antecedent.

(In sentence structures like this, *nine* functions as a pronoun. If the host had said *The Grammy nominations were announced today, and Beyoncé leads the Grammy nominees with nine*, then *nine* would have had an explicit referent and would function as an adjective.)

In the discussion that followed, people wondered whether the host misspoke by making a speech error when reading from the script or if my friend had misheard the report. Regardless of what was actually said, the sentence itself is linguistically interesting.

Most people would easily understand that statement. Analyzing the sentence pragmatically (that is, taking context into account), it's clear that although the reference to the concept of nominations isn't explicit, there is an implicit connection. Most members of NPR's audience share the following mutual knowledge:

- Beyoncé is a successful singer.
- Grammy awards are given to people in the music industry.
- Beyoncé has been a Grammy-award nominee in the past.
- NPR delivers news.
- This news piece in which this sentence was spoken involved Grammy-award nominees.
- If you are a nominee, you have been nominated for something.

This sentence also has ENTAILMENTS. A statement ENTAILS a second statement if the second statement is a consequence of the first statement. The statement *Daniel Radcliffe played the part of Harry Potter in several movies* entails the statement *Daniel Radcliffe exists*. That is, *Daniel Radcliffe exists* is a necessary consequence of the first statement. (*Daniel Radcliffe exists* is an entailment of *Daniel Radcliffe played the part of Harry Potter in several movies*.) Some entailments of the sentence *Beyoncé leads the Grammy nominees with nine* are:

- Beyoncé exists.
- Beyoncé has eight [nominations] (that is, having nine things entails having eight things).

Again, nine what? We assume that the radio host expects the audience to understand the statement. The audience assumes that the host is being relevant, so, listeners resort to context to fill in the gaps. Although the sentence could be argued to be grammatically ill-formed, context clues lead us to the conclusion that the missing antecedent is "nominations."

Contextually, there are other possible antecedents – "songs," perhaps. But, real world knowledge tells us that a person can also be nominated for albums, for example, or for production. Most other nouns and noun phrases that theoretically could be antecedents – chickens, tornadoes, sandwiches from Carnegie Deli – would complete the sentence and make it semantically well-formed but contextually odd.

Beyoncé leads the Grammy nominees with nine is not a grammatically well-formed sentence if there has been no reference to "nominations" in the prior discourse. However, it is a sentence that speakers who are aware of real-world conditions understand. They share the mutual knowledge that Grammys are won by singers, Beyoncé is a singer and a nominee, and most importantly that nominees have nominations.

That is to say, *Beyoncé leads the Grammy nominees with nine nominations* and *Beyoncé leads the Grammy nominees with nine chickens* are both well-formed sentences. However, only the first makes sense in context. This concept of "making sense in context" is called FELICITOUSNESS or FELICITY. We say that the first Beyoncé example is FELICITOUS and the second Beyoncé example is INFELICITOUS. In other words, *Beyoncé leads the Grammy nominees with nine chickens* is grammatically well-formed but infelicitous.

The linguist Herbert Clark analyzes how mutual knowledge among participants in a discourse can be used in creating novel uses of existing words. Words that are made up on the spot for a specific interpretation in a specific context are called NONCE words. ("Nonce" comes from the Middle English phrase "for the nones," which means "for the occasion.")

One example of this is the productive use of eponymous verb phrases. (An EPONYM is a word that is derived from a proper noun: the cocktail called the *manhattan* is named for the New York borough of Manhattan. The airship called a *zeppelin* is named for the German inventor Count Ferdinand von Zeppelin. Both *manhattan* and *zeppelin* are eponymous words. An *eponym* can also refer to the person something is named after.)

In Chapter 10 of his book *Arenas of Language Use*, Clark explains how the eponymous phrase *do a Napoleon* means different things in different contexts. In the context of wartime strategies, it would refer to perhaps surrendering or being exiled. In the context of having your photograph taken, it would refer to sticking one of your hands inside the front of your shirt. If you were unaware of the famous painting of Napoleon with his hand placed inside his shirt, you wouldn't know what was meant when a photographer told you to "do a Napoleon." For these meanings to be properly conveyed, the speaker would necessarily have to assume that their audience shared the same knowledge about the referent. (And the audience would have to assume that the speaker uttering such a statement is intending to be understood.)

Something you can do!

- Write down three different phrases in the frame "do an X" where X is a person's name.
- Compare them with your classmates to see if they understand the connection. Are the multiple possibilities? If necessary, you can provide additional context.

6.3 Conversational implicature[2]

Let's examine the sentence *Can you close the window?*

Taken literally, a person who utters this question is asking someone if they are physically capable of closing a window. However, most native speakers of English know that questions of the form "Can you do X?" are not about the ability of the person they're addressing. Rather, such questions are understood as polite requests to do something. The fact that these kinds of questions are actually polite requests and not questions of ability is a *convention* of the English language. Asking *Can you close the window?* is a polite way of expressing the command *Close the window*. There is nothing in the meaning inherent in these words that would yield this reading.

Something you can do!

- Write down five statements that implicate something other than what is literally meant.
- Compare your statements with those of your classmates.
- Do you see any patterns or similarities?

Here's another example of a sentence that implicates something more than what it literally means:

Kayla has two children.

If Kayla has three children, is the above sentence true? Yes, the sentence is still true – if someone has three children, then they also have two children. (It can also truthfully be said that Kayla has one child.) In other words, having three children entails having two children.

However, the conventional understanding of the sentence *Kayla has two children* is *Kayla has **two and only two** children*. By convention, upon hearing *Kayla has two children*, we would not assume Kayla has three children, unless there were a specific context that would cause us to believe that she did.

One more example of a sentence that implicates something more than what it literally means:

Have you been cheating on your diet?

This statement PRESUPPOSES that you have in fact been dieting. By virtue of answering the question "yes" or "no," you will implicate that you are on a diet.

In 1967, the philosopher H. Paul Grice delivered a series of lectures at Harvard University. One significant lecture first appeared in print in 1975. His lectures laid the foundation for the study of implicatures made in conversation that involve more than the meaning of what is said and take into account the situational context. Participants in a conversation adhere to what he calls the COOPERATIVE PRINCIPLE:

> "Make your conversational contribution such as is required, at the stage at which it occurs, by the accepted purpose or direction of the talk exchange in which you are engaged."

In order to have successful communication, participants must adhere to the Cooperative Principle, otherwise conversation breaks down.

6.3.1 Grice's maxims of conversation

In his article "Logic and Conversation," Grice formulates four conversational maxims for analyzing conversations.

Maxim #1: Quantity

1   Make your contribution as informative as is required (for the current purposes of the exchange.)
2   Do not make your contribution more informative that is required.

Maxim #2: Quality – Try to make your contribution one that is true;

1   Do not say what you believe to be false.
2   Do not say that for which you lack adequate evidence.

Maxim #3: Relation – Be relevant.

Maxim #4: Manner – Be perspicuous.

1   Avoid obscurity of expression.
2   Avoid ambiguity.
3   Be brief.
4   Be orderly.

In short: when communicating, say just enough but not more than what is necessary to be understood, using statements that are true, relevant, and easy to understand. Not adhering to these conversational principles can result in failure to be understood. This framework is helpful in analyzing breakdowns in communication. (Many linguists have found it rather amusing that Grice says "Be perspicuous" instead of "Express yourself clearly" in that using a fairly unfamiliar word instead of a more easily accessible phrase could itself be a violation of this maxim.)

Grice outlines four ways that you can fail to fulfill a maxim:

1   You intentionally *violate* a maxim. (Outright lying is an example of this.) Usually this results in misleading others.
2   You *opt out* of the Conversational Principle by literally stating that you're not cooperating. Grice offers "I cannot say more; my lips are sealed" as an example.
3   You face a *clash* – that is, you find impossible to fulfill one maxim without violating another.
4   You *flout* a maxim by not fulfilling it. If the audience assumes you're able to fulfill the maxim without a clash, are not opting out, are not misleading, and that you are observing the Cooperative Principle, then they will determine what you're trying to convey. In Grice's terminology, you are *exploiting* a maxim, and this is what gives rise to implicature.

6.3.2 Implicature

An IMPLICATURE is what you convey or implicate without literally and directing expressing it. (For example, the command "Open the window" is the implicature that arises from the question *Can you open the window?*)

To explain the three kinds of conversational implicature, Grice devised the following scenarios involving people named "A," "B," and "C":

- *Examples in which no maxim is violated.* A is standing by a disabled car and B approaches. A says "I'm out of gas." B responds "There's a station around the corner."

  B implicates that B thinks the gas station is probably open. (If B knew the gas station was closed, B would be flouting the maxim of Relation: B's statement would not be relevant.) If A and B are adhering to the Cooperative Principle, A would have no reason to believe B would be flouting the maxim of Relation. So, A understands that B intends A to think that A can get gas at that gas station and no longer be out of gas.

- *Examples in which a violation of a maxim is explained by the supposition of a clash of another maxim.* A is going on a vacation in France. A and B both know that A wants to visit C if it's not out of A's way. A asks *Where does C live?* B responds *Somewhere in the south of France.*

  A is seeking information about whether they can visit C. B's statement does not give A enough information to determine this. Because of that, B's answer could be thought to violate the first maxim of Quantity. (That is, B did not make their contribution informative enough.) But, A would not expect B to opt out of the Conversational Principle. So, A infers that if B were to be more specific, B would violate the maxim of Quality. (That is, if B were more specific, B might say something without having the evidence to back it up.) And because of that, A infers that B doesn't know the name of the town C lives in.

- *Examples that involve the flouting of a maxim.* Many figures of speech can be explained by this approach. A figure of speech is, by definition, not literal.

When you use the following rhetorical devices, you are flouting the first maxim of Quality because what is said is literally not true:

- IRONY – The use of the opposite literal meaning. (Example: uttering *I just love rainy days* when it's obvious to the audience that the utterer does not in fact love rainy days. By context, the audience knows that the utterer is not being literal.)

- METAPHOR – The use of comparison. (Example: *You are my sunshine.* Humans are obviously not sunshine. The utterer is comparing the audience to some of the attributes of sunshine.)
- MEIOSIS – The use of understatement. (Example: *He was a little unprepared* when used of one who completely bombed an interview. The utterer is using understatement to convey how badly the interview went.)
- HYPERBOLE – The use of exaggeration. (Example*: I could eat a thousand pizzas* when used by one who is very hungry. Obviously, a person could not eat a thousand pizzas.)

Situations where the first maxim of Quantity is flouted include:

- TAUTOLOGY – The use of redundancy. (Example: *People are people.*)
- Grice's "letter of recommendation" scenario: A professor ("A") is writing a recommendation for a student ("B"). The recommendation says only "A's command of English is excellent, and their attendance at tutorials has been regular." A is not opting out – because if A opted out, A could choose to not write a letter. As B's professor, A knows B's work. A knows more information is wanted. Therefore, A must wish to convey information that A cannot write down. This holds true only if one assumes that A feels B is no good – and that is what A is implicating. (Implicatures are culture-bound – there are cultures where succinct recommendations are the norm.)

As an example of flouting the maxim of Relation, Grice offers this scenario: A and B are talking. A insults C. B goes silent and then responds "The weather has been quite delightful this summer, hasn't it?" This obvious refusal to respond relevantly to the insult is an implicature that the A has made an inappropriate comment; or in Grice's words, A has "committed a social gaffe."

In the Beyoncé example, I stated that a necessary component of analyzing the interaction between the host and the audience was that the audience had to assume to that the host was being relevant.

Without the assumption that communication is relevant, communication breaks down.

Grice lists ambiguity, obscurity, and failure to be succinct as examples of flouting the maxim of Manner. He compares the following two phrases that a reviewer might write: "X sang *Home Sweet Home*" and "X produced a series of sounds that corresponded closely with the score of *Home Sweet Home*." With this second example, the reviewer implicates that the performance is flawed.

6.3.3 Reformulations of Grice's maxims

Since the late 1960s and early 1970s when Grice developed these maxims, linguists like Laurence Horn, Stephen Levinson, Deirdre Wilson, and Dan Sperber have reformulated Grice's basic tenets.[3]

Horn's theoretical framework involves a two-pronged approach:

- Q-Principle: Say as much as you can.
- R-Principle: Say no more than you must.

Levinson has a three-pronged framework from which he derives three principles (which he calls *heuristics*):

- First heuristic: What isn't said, isn't.
- Second heuristic: What is simply described is stereotypically exemplified.
- Third heuristic: What is said in an abnormal way isn't normal.

Wilson and Sperber have conflated all of Grice's maxims into one overarching maxim: Relevance.

6.4 Speech acts

You can use words to convey something other than what those words mean. Also, you can *do* things with words. You can cause people to be married, declare someone guilty or not guilty, or christen a ship.

For these statements to have an effect, you must meet the criteria by which these words can have that effect. The study of what you can do with words by means of communicating them is called SPEECH ACT THEORY. The genesis of this theory comes from John Austin's *How To Do Things With Words*.

Austin analyzes what is brought about through communication.

- A LOCUTIONARY ACT is the literal performance of an utterance – the production of speech sounds in such a way to create coherent words that form coherent sentences and phrases that have actual semantic meaning. A LOCUTION is what is said.
- An ILLOCUTIONARY ACT is the intended meaning conveyed by the utterance. An ILLOCUTION is the meaning of what is said.
- A PERLOCUTIONARY ACT is the action that takes effect because of what is said. A PERLOCUTION is the result of what is said.

Let's return to the question *Can you close the window*? The locutionary act is the literal utterance of those words. The meaning conveyed by the illocutionary act is "Close the window." The perlocutionary act is causing someone to close the window by the uttering of those words.

Utterances that change reality by their having been communicated are called PERFORMATIVES. By uttering a promise (a locutionary act), you intend to make a promise (the illocutionary act), and by having uttered it, you have made a promise (the perlocutionary act). A promise is a performative utterance.[4]

Something you can do!

- Examine statements like "I now pronounce you to be married." or "I declare tomorrow to be a holiday." What are the illocutionary and perlocutionary effects of these statements? What conditions need to be true in order for the perlocutionary effects to take place? Provide two other statements whose intended meaning is different from their actual semantic meaning.

Knowledge of speech act theory gives you the tools to analyze the effects of a speaker's words on others.

For example, a politician can persuade their followers to volunteer their time for the public good or incite them to commit violence. Bigots can use words (called DOG-WHISTLES) that have an innocent, straightforward meaning that seems harmless or unthreatening, but which have a specific hateful meaning to other bigots. In such case, what the speaker says is distinct from what the speaker intends.

6.5 Discourse analysis

Instead of analyzing each statement in a conversation in isolation, DISCOURSE ANALYSIS involves examining the conversation as a whole and determining how each utterance made in sequence (called a TURN) relates to the conversation and the social interaction as a whole.

Something you can do!

- Get permission from two of your friends to record a 30-second stretch of their conversation. (You might wish to let them speak a little first and then take a 30-second chunk after they're in the middle of the conversation). Transcribe their speech, including all the starts, stops, ums, etc.
- In what ways does their speech form complete grammatical sentences?
- In what ways do they not speak in full grammatical sentences?
- What patterns do you notice as they go back and forth?

Observable conventions in conversation are less likely to change over time than, for example, the individual units of speech sounds. Still, conventions do change.

When you say "Thank you," to older people, perhaps you find the response "You're welcome" to be cold or off-putting, and perhaps they find the more recent use of "No worries" to be flippant. Do you think there been a shift away from "You're welcome" to "No worries" in recent times?

Examine the turns of dialog in answering a phone call. Calls once routinely began like this:

RECIPIENT OF CALL: "Hello?" (A question, indicating that the recipient has answered the call and is inquiring who is calling.)

CALLER (if known to the recipient): "Hello." (A statement, by which the recipient will recognize the voice and know who is calling.) If the caller is unsure that the recipient will recognize their voice, they would say something like "Hello. It's Morgan."

Compare that with modern-day phone calls, when the recipient will know who is calling from caller ID or because the caller's number is programmed into the recipient's phone. The recipient, rather than asking "Hello?" as a question, will know who is calling and will generally start with "Hello." as a statement. Or, the recipient can dive right in: "What?", "Hello, Dr. Reynolds," "I'm on my way," etc.[5]

Discourse is not limited to the spoken or signed communication. Discourse can also be written. Linguists have been analyzing real-time written conversation in as far back as the 1990s when people first began hanging out in chatrooms.

The ability to communicate via text messaging changes the discourse framework. Participants in a text conversation cannot see or hear each other, so they lack cues like vocal intonation and body language that indicate the speaker's mood and intent. For example, it can be harder to tell if a simple statement that's been texted is meant sincerely or sarcastically, and you might have a harder time determining if your audience has taken in what you've communicated in the way that you've intended. One way people offer context cues for intent is through the use of emoji.

Another change brought about by texting involves punctuation. Linguists have analyzed how communicating by text have changed something as simple as ending a declarative sentence with a period. A sentence-final period in a text can be taken as a sign of hostility, snark, or passive-aggressiveness, and so periods are often left out in text. Others use exclamation points to avoid the hostility associated with the period.[6]

Something you can do!

- Examine a string of text messages that you've recently exchanged with a friend.
- Describe how this conversation differs from spoken conversation.
- Describe how it differs from conversation that you might see written in a book or other formalized form of writing. (If you discuss this in class or with other people, make sure you get permission from your friend to do so.)
- What emoji were used? How did those emoji help signal intent?

Even little words like *oh, you know, well*, and *um* (collectively known as DISCOURSE MARKERS) have important roles in the analysis of conversation. Andreas Jucker, a linguist who studies historical pragmatics, has examined discourse markers like *well* stretching back to Old English, where it was used to get the attention of the audience, as at the start of a concluding statement. In his article "Pragmatics and Language Change: Historical Pragmatics," Jucker cites the use of *well* in Middle English in Chaucer's *Canterbury Tales*, where it is used with reported speech to indicate "that the speaker whose speech is reported accepts a certain situation." And by the early Modern English period in the 1600s, he reports that *well* has begun to be used to lessen the degree to which an utterance could be seen as threatening or negative to the hearer.

Mitigating potentially threatening interactions leads us to the topic of politeness.

6.6 Politeness

Politeness theory involves strategies that protect an individual's public self-image in a social interaction, including conversation. Your public self-image is referred to as your FACE. People use many strategies to protect their face from face-threatening acts. Much of politeness theory is based on the early work of Penelope Brown and Stephen Levinson and their book *Politeness*.

A direct command could potentially be threatening to a person's face. Politeness minimizes the degree of the threat. One way to make a command within minimal threat to face is to employ what Brown and Levinson call the indirect strategy, which involves the maxims of conversation discussed earlier in the chapter. Saying *It's really hot in here* carries the implication that the speaker would like the hearer to undertake an action, such as turning on the air conditioning or opening a window, and in making this utterance, the speaker avoids the threat of a direct command like *Open the window!*

Something you can do!

- Pair up with a classmate or study partner.
- Discuss how you would interact with another person if:

    - you wanted that person to open a window
    - you wanted to buy a cup of coffee or tea
    - you needed to apologize for bumping into them
    - you wanted to sit in an empty seat next to them on a train

- Describe ways that your conversational strategies are alike or different.

Certain parts of the United States are viewed as more polite than others. (Compare popularly held attitudes about the southern United States to New York City, for example.) Politeness hierarchies vary greatly from region to region and country to country. Businesspeople in foreign countries must learn the conventions of their host country if they don't wish to unintentionally offend others.

In the past several decades in the United States, there has been a marked shift in formality. When you reader older books or watch older movies, you see that far fewer people were on a first-name basis. Honorifics and surnames were much more common. Teachers would address students as Master Thomas or Miss Williams; doctors would address patients as Mr. Jefferson, or Mrs. Wilson.

During the transition from very formal to less formal modes of address, many people were insulted by the perceived lack of formality and found this presumption to be impolite. Nowadays, very few people think twice when your barista calls you by your first name when you've ordered a coffee.

Also in terms of addressing people, in recent years, a greater effort is made to address people in the way they wish to be addressed. Instead of making assumptions based on outward appearance whether an individual is to be referred to as *he* or *she*, many institutions (such as healthcare providers and schools) will ask individuals what set of pronouns they use: *he/him, she/her, they/them*, or another set. (See section 4.2.5 for more discussion on pronoun use and the gender binary.)

In journalism, in the late 1900s there was a movement toward a "person first" approach. For example, you wouldn't refer to a person as "an anorexic," but rather as "a person with anorexia." More recently, it's been pointed out that these person-first rules can be disrespectful to individuals if you don't allow for a loosening of the style rules to allow people to identify themselves in the way they prefer. This approach is called PERSON CENTERED, and it embraces respect and empathy as key factors.[7]

6.7 Word order

As English uses fewer inflections, word order is more fixed. In standard word order, you say sentences like *Martin likes spaghetti.* When you intentionally change the word order, you're implying something different. Following the Conversational Principle, if you're not communicating in the most straightforward way possible; you must have a reason for it. The loss of inflectional endings over time has given rise not only to rigidity in word order, but also to the ability to change up the word order for pragmatic effect.

In earlier forms of English, you could say the equivalent of things like *Spaghetti Martin likes* or *Likes Martin spaghetti*. In today's English, there are no inflectional endings to indicate that *Martin* is the subject and *spaghetti* is the object. Your audience relies on adherence to word order, and would normally expect you would say *Martin likes spaghetti*. So if you use a different word order (and possibly a Yoda-like intonation) and utter *Spaghetti Martin likes* you convey the meaning *It's spaghetti that Martin likes* or *What Martin likes is spaghetti*.

The moving of the grammatical object is to the beginning of the sentence has been called PREPOSING. "It's spaghetti that Martin likes" is an example of a syntactic structure called an IT-CLEFT. And structures that front adverbial phrases that begin with words like *who, what, where*, and *how* (like "Where Chris likes to travel is India" or "Who Lee told the secret to is Pat") are called WH-CLEFTS.

In highly inflected languages with fluid word order, word order plays an important role in what you're trying to convey. Without taking context into account, Czech is categorized as an SVO language. But in conversation and prose, word order is much freer because Czech is a highly inflected language. One pragmatic effect is that new information is often placed at the end of the sentence.

Given these four Czech words:

žena	"queen" nominative case
kočce	"cat" dative case
rybu	"fish" accusative case
dala	"give" third person singular feminine past tense

there are many possible combinations.

In *Žena dala kočce rybu*, what's new to the discourse is "the fish." We might express this in English with constructions like *What the woman gave to the cat was a fish* or *It was a fish that the woman gave to the cat*.

In *Rybu kočce dala žena*, the new discourse item is "the woman." This could be in expressed in English with constructions like *Who gave the fish to the cat was the woman* or *It was the woman who gave the fish to the cat*.

For languages like English with a more fixed word order, the act of deviating from standard word order causes the audience to make inferences as to why the deviation is made. For languages like Czech with a freer word order, word order itself is a feature of the discourse. Determining the new information to the discourse doesn't rely as much on inference.

6.8 Conclusion

In this chapter, we've looked at ways that the meaning you convey is more than the meaning of the words you use. We've discussed reference and context. We've analyzed how conversations are structured. Assuming that people we communicate with adhere to the Cooperative Principle allows us to flout conversational maxims to create implicatures that show what we intend, even though it might not be explicitly apparent from the semantic meaning of what we say.

In the next chapter, we'll look at the influence of society and culture on language.

6.9 Questions for discussion

- How could you get someone to shut a door to a room without literally saying *Shut the door*?
- What is the Cooperative Principle?
- Someone who is authorized to perform marriages can cause two people to be married by saying, in the proper context, "I now pronounce you married." What are other things that can be accomplished by making a statement? What factors have to be met in order for that statement to have weight?
- What behaviors that are considered polite where you live, are considered rude in other parts of the world?
- Why is politeness important?

Notes

1 Further Reading: Barbara Abbott, "Reference."
2 Section 6.3 is adapted from "Have Your Salt and Eat It, Too," an article I wrote for *Verbatim: The Language Quarterly* (Volume 25, number 1, pages 20–23) in 2000. Grice's maxims are taken from his article "Logic and Conversation."
3 Further Reading: Larry Horn, "Toward a New Taxonomy for Pragmatic Inference"; Stephen Levinson, *Presumptive Meanings*; Dan Sperber and Deirdre Wilson, *Relevance*.
4 Further Reading: John Searle, "How Performatives Work."
5 Further Reading: Deborah Schiffrin, Deborah Tannen, and Heidi E. Hamilton (editors), *The Handbook of Discourse Analysis*; Deborah Tannen, *Conversational Style* and *Gender and Discourse*.
6 Further Reading: Dan Bilefsky, "Period. Full Stop. Point. Whatever It's Called, It's Going Out of Style" (online access at https://nytimes.com/2016/06/10/world/europe/period-full-stop-point-whatever-its-called-millennials-arent-using-it.html); Rich Ling and Naomi S. Baron, "Text Messaging and IM: Linguistic Comparison of American College Data" (online access at http://american.edu/cas/lfs/faculty-docs/upload/text-messaging-and-im.pdf).
7 Further Reading: Alex Kapitan, "On 'Person-First Language': It's Time to Actually Put the Person First" (online access at https://radicalcopyeditor.com/2017/07/03/person-centered-language/).

Chapter 7

Society and culture

7.0 Introduction

Each of the previous chapters was an overview of a linguistic subfield and examined how English has changed in that subfield.

This chapter deals with SOCIOLINGUISTICS, the study of the influence of society and culture on language, including the way society and culture cause language change. Sociolinguists analyze the phonological, morphological, syntactic, semantic, or pragmatic features of one or more social groups (such as ones categorized by gender, economic class, race, ethnicity, or age). Some sociolinguists document how these linguistic features are manifested in the speech of a particular social group, others compare and contrast similarities and differences across multiple groups, still others document linguistic changes that certain groups innovate.

Obviously, no social or cultural group is a monolithic entity. The phonological features of the working class in Pittsburgh are different from those of the working class in Manchester, Baltimore, or Adelaide, and these phonological features change over time.

REGIONAL VARIATION (also called DIALECTOLOGY) is the study of how a language varies from region to region. For languages spoken worldwide like English, the analysis can be global or within a country: for example, documenting a variety of English spoken in the bayous of Louisiana, or comparing English spoken in southwestern England to that of Yorkshire.

7.1 Language and variety

Imagine two people speaking to each other. Could you tell if they're speaking the same language, different dialects of the same language, or different languages? Let's examine what this question means.

A LANGUAGE is a system of communicating thoughts by using vocal sounds, written symbols, gestures, or other arbitrary forms, as used by a nation, people, or other community. *Language* is used in contrast with VARIETY or DIALECT, a subset of a language used by a specific population, usually in a specific region, in a way that is considered distinct from other populations who use that language. For example, the French spoken in Québec City is a variety of French. The English spoken in the southern Appalachian region of the United States is a variety of English.

The varieties of a language can differ in terms of their phonology, morphology, syntax, vocabulary, and pragmatics. For example: in many English varieties, [r] is dropped after vowels, so that *card* is pronounced [kɑ:d] instead of [kɑrd]. (When varieties differ phonologically, often speakers of the varieties other than the one that's considered standard are said to have an accent.) In Parisian French, *éventuellement* means "maybe"; in Canadian French, it means "eventually." Syntactic examples include *need + Xing* verbal constructions and the use of double modals, as covered in section 4.3.4. Varieties aren't static: like all living languages, they change over time.

Some linguists distinguish the term *variety* from *dialect*, and others do not. When these two terms are distinguished, it's sometimes in recognition of the fact that some people hold the negative judgment that a dialect is less important or less correct than "full-fledged" or "official" languages. The use of *dialect* in this book is neutral of value judgments.

A language is generally associated with a specific country, a group of countries, or a specific people. If a language is associated with a specific people, members of this population might live primarily in one country, or this speech community might be spread across many countries. Some countries have one official language and some have several. Many countries have not designated an official language.

With this background, let's return to the question of whether you could determine if two people are speaking the same language.

If two speakers cannot understand each other at all, they are probably speaking different languages. But, maybe not. Maybe one speaks a heavily accented local variety: for example, many Americans find it hard to understand some varieties of English spoken in Scotland. The characters in the 1996 movie *Trainspotting* used a regional variety of English that's spoken in Edinburgh, where the story is set. When this movie was released in the United States, the actors redubbed some of the scenes to aid comprehension by an American audience.[1]

If two speakers can understand each other, they are probably speaking the same language. But, maybe not. Many Czechs and Slovaks understand each other. (If speakers of two languages can understand each other, these languages are said to be MUTUALLY INTELLIGIBLE.) The syntax and the morphological inflections of Czech and Slovak are very similar, and much (but not all) of their vocabulary is very similar. Differences in their phonological systems are relatively minor and follow consistent patterns. Czech and Slovak are two different languages in the West Slavic family; they were even considered separate languages when Czechoslovakia was one country for most of the period between 1918 and 1989.

A DIALECT CHAIN (also called a DIALECT CONTINUUM) is a series of language varieties spread over a region where geographically adjacent varieties are mutually intelligible. The greater the number of intervening dialects that geographically separate two dialects at far ends of the chain, the less likely speakers will be able to understand each other. Generally speaking, Czechs in eastern Czech Republic and Slovaks in western Slovakia have an easier time understanding each other than people of western Czech Republic and eastern Slovakia.

The degree that speakers are open to differences also plays into whether two people speaking mutually intelligible languages will actually understand each other. Speakers who are open to differences can use context cues to help decode the differences. At the other extreme, two people from nations or regions at war with each other might not be open to the difference and fail to understand one another.

Whether a communication system is classified as a language or dialect often involves political power or lack thereof. The linguist Max Weinreich is attributed with the popularization of the saying "A language is a dialect with an army and a navy." Catalan, spoken in northeastern Spain and southeastern France, is a Romance language that is linguistically distinct from Spanish. For many decades, particularly under Francisco Franco's reign (1939–1975) as Spain's military dictator, government officials in Spain claimed that Catalan was a dialect of Spanish, and not a language in its own right. People in Spain who spoke languages other than Spanish were seen as a threat to national stability. The suppression of languages spoken by linguistic minorities is one tactic undertaken by oppressive regimes to establish authority.

Typically, a variety is categorized as standard if it lacks stigmatized features. A stigmatized variety of a language is sometimes referred to as a VERNACULAR. Vernaculars are often associated with varieties used by members of lower socioeconomic classes and ethnic or racial minorities. Even though vernacular varieties have their own consistent set of grammatical, phonological, and morphological rules, racist or classist attitudes by speakers of standard varieties result in negative judgment of those who speak vernacular varieties. Sociolinguists have shown that these vernaculars are just as linguistically robust and valid as nonstigmatized varieties of speech, yet prejudice against such vernaculars and their speakers is common.

The term Standard English is a misnomer because it implies there is one single variety of English that is standard; there isn't.

7.2 Language contact

The field of LANGUAGE CONTACT (or CONTACT LINGUISTICS) examines what happens when groups of speakers from two different languages come in contact with each other. Language contact is a critical component in the study of the history of language development.

For example, the Norman Conquest in 1066 brought large numbers of speakers of Norman French into England. This contact changed English considerably. Over the next couple of centuries, Latinate words (via French) were infused into English. Sometimes these words replaced the equivalent word in English altogether.

Sometimes a Norman French word was added to the vocabulary of English, perhaps with a slight change in meaning. For example, *sheep* is an Old English word. (The *Oxford English Dictionary* has a citation for it in an Old English form, *scepa*, dating to around 825 CE.) *Mutton* comes from the French word for sheep *mouton*. The Anglo-Normans used *mouton* (in a variety of attested spellings) for "sheep." By 1300, the word *mutton* in English came to refer to the meat of the sheep. Other "animal"/"meat of the animal" English/Norman French pairings include *cow/beef* and *pig/pork*.

A more recent example is the development of International Sign. Sign languages are different from country to country. For example, although English is spoken in both the United States and the United Kingdom, the two sign languages associated with these countries, American Sign Language and British Sign Language, are mutually unintelligible. (In fact, because the development of American Sign Language in the early 1800s was influenced by French Sign Language, ASL has much more in common with FSL than it does with BSL.) As members of the Deaf community have come together in recent decades at international conferences and sporting events, this has led to the genesis of International Sign.[2]

7.2.1 Pidgins and creoles

A PIDGIN is a form of communication between two (or more) groups who have come into contact and do not speak any language in common. Sometimes the contact is peaceful, as between merchants traveling far from their home and the people they trade with. Often the contact is in a more violent context, as during war or as the result of enslavement. Pidgins have developed for communication between conquering forces and the peoples they've conquered. Pidgins have also developed for communication among conquered peoples who speak different languages.

A pidgin is not spoken by any of its speakers as a native language. It includes vocabulary from the source languages. The syntax is very simple. Complex morphological features from the source languages are simplified and flattened. (International Sign, discussed above, is considered an example of a pidgin.)

The traditional definition of a CREOLE is a language that is spoken as a native language by a descendent of a person who speaks a pidgin and is not one of the contact languages contributing to that pidgin. Most sociolinguists believe that most creoles develop from pidgins. Other sociolinguists maintain that creoles develop from the direct mixing of languages and that pidgins are not involved. Either way, creoles *are* languages and are not "simplified" or "broken" languages. Theorists who assert that creoles develop from pidgins recognize that creoles are as complex as languages that don't derive from pidgins (although some argue that creoles tend to lack the very elaborate phonological, morphological, and syntactic features that develop over long periods of time).

The period of European colonialization that began with the voyages of Christopher Columbus in 1492 ushered in widespread linguistic change across the globe. Conquerors imposed their European languages, especially English, Spanish, Portuguese, French, and Dutch, upon indigenous populations and populations of enslaved Africans.

Enslaved peoples from different parts of western Africa spoke different languages from several different language groups, apparently mostly in the Niger-Congo family. The contact among these languages and those spoken by Europeans engaged in the slave trade gave rise to pidgins. Some of these pidgins developed into creoles spoken in Africa, and probably some of these pidgins were brought to the Americas and developed into creoles there.

Many indigenous peoples of the Caribbean islands were annihilated, and little documentation of indigenous languages spoken during that period exists. Although many languages became extinct, some of the vocabulary was incorporated into that of the European colonizers and the creoles that had developed from the contact of European and African languages. A few words from indigenous Caribbean languages made it back to Europe, particularly to describe Caribbean flora and fauna that didn't exist in Europe.

Of course, the development of pidgins and creoles is not limited to the Caribbean. The contact stemming from the travel of Europeans to southeastern Asia and India, of Chinese to the Malay Archipelago, and of Europeans and North Americans in Oceania, are other examples of contact that led to the creation of pidgins and creoles.

Historically, creoles often have been stigmatized. Many countries have undertaken steps to instill pride in using indigenous creoles. Some countries have a creole as an official language, like Haitian Creole (*kreyòl ayisyen*), which is spoken in Haiti. Many speakers of creoles are bilingual, speaking the official language of their region in addition to a creole. (Some speakers learn both languages natively as children, others learn the official language when they begin school or join the workforce.)

In recent decades, lexicographers have compiled dictionaries for many creoles. Richard Allsop's *Dictionary of Caribbean Usage*, first published in 1996, is an important reference work that documents the vocabulary of many different varieties of English and English Creole spoken in the Caribbean. Other reference works document the lexicon of a specific country, like Lise Winer's *Dictionary of the English/ Creole of Trinidad & Tobago*.[3]

7.2.2 *African American English*

Some varieties are spoken predominantly by members of a particular racial or ethnic group, although not every member does.

In the United States, African American English (AAE) is such an example. Although African Americans are not a monolithic community, there are phonological, morphological, and syntactic patterns, along with lexical items, that many African Americans use, many of which are not features of other varieties of American English. AAE is also referred to by several other names, including African Amercian Vernacular English. Lisa Green's introduction to her textbook *African American English* lists these names and explains why sociolinguists have adopted particular names over others.

Regarding the development of AAE, one theory is that it is structurally related to the Niger-Congo languages of West Africa and developed in the United States as a creole. This view is known as the CREOLIST POSITION. A contrasting view, known as the DIALECTOLOGIST (or ANGLICIST) POSITION is that the distinctive features of AAE are related to forms found in historical varieties of English and in varieties in the Southern United States that early speakers of AAE were in contact with.[4]

Regardless of the origins of AAE, sociolinguists agree that its phonology, morphology, and syntax is as rule-based as those of standard varieties of English. AAE is not broken English, a lesser form of English, or improper English. The title of Geoffrey Pullum's article "African American Vernacular English Is Not Standard English with Mistakes" speaks for itself. For example, Pullum states that a common misconception about AAE made by people who don't speak AAE is that the copula (the verb *be* and its forms *am, is, are, was, were, being, been*) "is carelessly omitted or is used in incorrect forms out of ignorance." In fact, there are detailed, specific rules regarding when the copula can be omitted; Pullum lists 10 such rules. Often when people who don't speak AAE try to imitate it, they will drop *be* and its forms in contexts that a speaker of AAE naturally would not. Pullum goes on to describe several other syntactic features and how they are consistently applied according to the syntactic rules of AAE.

Spoken Soul, by John Russell Rickford and Russell John Rickford, is another resource that explores the vocabulary, pronunciation, grammar, and history of AAE, its role in American society, and "the vibrancy and vitality of Spoken Soul as an expressive instrument in American literature, religion, entertainment, and everyday life."

7.2.3 Linguistic minorities

Linguistic minorities – people whose native language is not the official language of their country – are found across the world. Many are bilingual. Those who are not bilingual often face the economic hardships associated with not being able to communicate in the governmentally sanctioned language.

In France, the *Académie française* dictates what is Standard French (which is based on a variety of Parisian French) and what is not. But, Parisian French is just one variety of French. Not all citizens of France speak it. In the south of France, the languages of several speech communities fall under the umbrella of Occitan. (The Old Provençal word for "yes" is *oc* – as opposed to French *oui* – and there is a linguistic divide between *langue d'oc* and *langue d'oïl* – the latter being the basis for standard Modern French.)

The languages of the Occitan region, which share similarities with Catalan and Italian, could be categorized as another subbranch of the Romance branch on the Indo-European tree, in which case they would not be varieties of French but varieties of Occitan (for which there is no one standard form). In this region, populations are pressured to learn standard French. Many of the varieties are on the verge of dying out. Linguists are cataloging them so that they're not permanently lost, and in some cases local schools are keeping them alive.

In Ireland, Irish Gaelic is now commonly taught in schools and there's a Welsh revival in Wales. In the United States, Canada, and Australia, there are movements to document, protect, encourage the use of, and revitalize indigenous languages that have not yet died out.

As you will recall from Chapter 1, no one knows how exactly how many languages have become extinct. Many languages today are on the verge of extinction. The Endangered Languages Project is an important resource, serving as "an online resource for samples and research on endangered languages as well as a forum for advice and best practices for those working to strengthen linguistic diversity."

Something you can do!

- Go to the Endangered Languages Project website (endangeredlanguages.com).
- Choose a language that you've never heard of.
- Prepare a brief presentation about this language, including where it's spoken, how many people speak it, why it's endangered, and what measures are being taken to keep it from becoming extinct.
- Share your presentation with your classmates.

7.3 Variation among social groups

Sociolinguists study and document how members of a social group use the language differently than nonmembers. These differences can involve a variety of linguistic elements, including vocabulary, sentence structure, inflectional endings, or pronunciation. Sometimes the differences are intentional, and the speaker embraces them as a means of identifying with that particular group. Other times, speakers are unaware of these distinctions.

To conduct research ethically, you must gain the consent of the person you're interviewing. Since the person being recorded is aware that they're being recorded and listened to, that awareness can affect their speech. The research of the influential sociologist Erving Goffman on face-to-face interaction is critical to the field. In *Behavior in Public Places*, he explains how people modify the way they present themselves (including speech) depending on whether they're being observed and who they're being observed by. Because people modify their speech (whether consciously or unconsciously) when they're being observed, researchers will often record longer stretches of dialogs, ask open-ended questions, and establish good rapport to minimize these effects. Some researchers, but not all, will tell informants after an interview what features of their speech are being analyzed.

Something you can do!

- List social groups that you are a member of.
- In what ways do you use language differently than people who are not also members of this group?
- What accounts for differences in the way different social groups speak English?
- How do you feel when you meet someone who uses English differently than you do?

In answering the second question, do you feel that you speak differently in certain situations? Do you talk differently to your teachers or supervisors than you do to your friends? Most people can communicate in multiple registers. A REGISTER is a variety of language spoken in a specific context. Someone with the BBC in London might speak a prestige variety like Received Pronunciation at work, and a more informal variety when out at the pub with friends. Someone who says *Me and her are gonna go to the beach* to a friend might write *She and I will go to the conference* in a work email. These are examples of people using different registers based on their audience.

You should consider multiple variables when comparing different groups of speakers. If you're studying vowel shifts and are trying to determine which social groups are innovators, you can't just compare women's vowel production to men's. You'd want to test other variables, too: whether black women and men and white women and men have shifted similarly, whether there are different results based on age, whether socioeconomic status and education levels have an effect, and so forth. The more variables you're accounting for, the more informants you need.

One reason that sociolinguists document and describe language as it is actually spoken (and written) is to show that all varieties follow their own internal structure, and that even though there are prestige varieties, linguistically they are no different than stigmatized ones. Sociologists also work to dispel misconceptions that are held about the way different groups of people use language.

For example, differences in the way women and men hold conversations have long caught the public interest. Many pop psychology books examine gender-based interactions to instruct readers how to improve failing relationships or workplace communication.

VOCAL FRY (also called CREAKY VOICE) occurs when a speaker loosely compresses the vocal folds while producing sound, resulting in a lower-pitched voice that has a rough, creaky or popping sound. In the mid-2010s, many news programs and articles criticized vocal fry as used by young women. Some people claimed vocal fry made women seem less professional or could jeopardize women's job prospects.[5]

However, linguistic research shows that vocal fry *isn't* solely the dominion of young women. Men employ it frequently as well. In response to the vocal fry backlash, linguistics professor Penelope Eckert stated on NPR's *Fresh Air* in 2015:

> The biggest users of vocal fry traditionally have been men, and it still is; men in the U.K., for instance. And it's considered kind of a sign of hyper-masculinity . . . and by the same token, uptalk, it's clear that in some people's voices that has really become a style, but it has been around forever, and people use it stylistically in a variety of ways – both men and women.[6]

Eckert explained that women's voices (especially those of younger women) were being criticized and men weren't being held to the same standard. Vocal fry had become another weapon used to demean women and women's contributions.

Vocal fry isn't a gender-based difference, but that message wasn't consistently delivered, due in part to sexism and the media's attempt to attract an audience by convincing people they're doing something wrong. (You've been eating bananas incorrectly! Butter is bad for you! Wait, no it's not!) As with other science reporting, when linguistic topics are in the news, facts aren't always adequately conveyed. At best, research is overly simplified for the audience. At worst, findings are misrepresented or important points are omitted.

So, can broad gender-based linguistic distinctions be made? In the area of phonology, it has been claimed that women tend to have higher-pitched voices than men. But, research by Erwan Pépiot shows that even though the pitch of women who speak American English is higher than that of men, this is not true of all languages. His findings suggest that pitch differences between men and women are language dependent and, in part, socially constructed.[7] For example, Japanese women have traditionally been enculturated to have higher-pitched voices.[8]

William Labov was an early pioneer in sociological field research. (In the 1960s, he analyzed variation in New York City by visiting department stores patronized by different economic classes. He would elicit the phrase "fourth floor" from employees by asking where to find a product that he knew was sold on the fourth floor. He paid attention to vowel quality and the degree to which the *r* was pronounced or dropped.[9])

Labov's influential 1990 paper, "The Intersection of Sex and Social Class in the Course of Linguistic Change," incorporates research from many important sociolinguistic works like *Jocks and Burnouts: Social Categories and Identities in the High School* and the article "The Whole Woman: Sex and Gender Differences in Variation," both by Penelope Eckert. Labov analyzes linguistic innovation with respect to gender and social class and summarizes the shifts in the prevailing viewpoints going back to the late 1800s. His research leads him to formulate two principles (in his words):

1   "In stable sociolinguistic stratification, men use a higher frequency of nonstandard forms than women."

2   "In the majority of linguistic changes, women use a higher frequency of the incoming forms than men." (Another way of saying this is "women are generally the innovators of linguistic change.")

But, Labov states, these principles don't fit into larger frameworks that account for gender differences, are hard to reconcile with each other, contradict established linguistic principles of change, and create conceptual problems. This brief description of Labov's paper greatly oversimplifies a complex phenomenon worthy of a semester-long course. His article is written at a level that should be generally understandable with the background you've gotten from this book. Students intrigued by this topic are encouraged to seek it out.

One area where gender plays a significant role is discourse analysis. (This topic is examined in detail in the works of Deborah Tannen, including *Gender and Discourse* and *Conversational Style*.) In a study by Adrienne Hancock and Benjamin Rubin and reported in their paper "Influence of Communication Partner's Gender on Language," they paired 40 people (20 women and 20 men) with conversation partners. Although they didn't find significant gender-based communication differences, it was the case that participants (both men and women) interrupted more when they were speaking with a woman.

7.4 Regional variation

The study of variation within a language in different places where it is spoken is known as REGIONAL VARIATION or DIALECTOLOGY. Some dialectologists compare and contrast language features among regions. Other dialectologists document or track changes that occur within a specific region. The linguistic features most commonly analyzed by dialectologists are phonological and semantic ones. This is not surprising. As we have seen, change occurs in these areas more rapidly than they do in syntax and morphology.

In section 5.3.2, we looked briefly at regional variation in word choice. A REGIONALISM is something that is particular to a specific geographical area. Linguistically, this would include words and pronunciations. For example, *soda, pop, soft drink,* and *tonic* are all regionalisms in the United States for a flavored, carbonated beverage. *American Tongues*, a popular PBS documentary produced in 1988, features spoken examples of many varieties of American English. You can watch it at pbs.org/pov/americantongues.

7.4.1 Dialect atlases and regional dictionaries

Since the late 1800s, information about regional differences has been published in dialect atlases. The area covered in such atlases can be an entire country or a smaller area within a country. The maps in these atlases show how linguistic features are distributed across an area. The first dialect atlases were produced for Germany, France, and India.

In the United States, beginning in the late 1920s, the Modern Language Association appointed the linguist Hans Kurath to compile what would become a series of reference works that are together known as the *Linguistic Atlas of the United States*. The first in this series, the *Linguistic Atlas of New England*, was published in 1939.[10]

In the United Kingdom, *The Linguistic Atlas of England* was first published in 1978, led by the editorial team of Harold Orton, Stewart Sanderson, and John Widdowson.

Something you can do!

- The *Dialect Atlas of Newfoundland and Labrador*, available at dialectatlas.mun.ca, documents "the geographical (and to some degree social) distribution of many features of the traditional dialects of English spoken in the Canadian province of Newfoundland and Labrador." Go to this website, browse the content of this atlas, and take some of its quizzes on comprehensibility.

  For example: select the entire province, and under the Category of Grammar, select the grammatical feature "Past forms of SEE". The map will show you where speakers use SEEN for SAW ("I never seen it.") and where speakers use SEED or SEE instead of SAW ("He see(d) you come.") Such tools can be helpful in analyzing patterns of a region.

- Look at two other grammatical features on this site. Discuss the results with your classmates. How does the variety of speech patterns compare to your own variety (or varieties) of speech?

Regional dictionaries document the lexicon as it is used in specific regions of a country. Although maps are an important feature, the content is generally arranged like a dictionary, with entries in alphabetical order, definitions, and labels that indicate where the words are commonly spoken. In the United States, the primary regional dictionary is *The Dictionary of American Regional English* (*DARE* for short). *DARE* "documents words, phrases, and pronunciations that vary from one place to another across the United States."

Work on *DARE* began in the early 1960s under the direction of Frederic Cassidy (and, after his retirement, Joan Houston Hall) at the University of Wisconsin–Madison. During the phase where information was gathered, linguists, a contingent of graduate students, and other volunteers interviewed people throughout the United States. In these interviews, the linguists would ask the informants what words they called various objects, paying attention to word choice and pronunciation.[11] For example, many informants read a short story called "Arthur the Rat" so that researchers could get examples of specific phonological representations from all over the country. Recordings of people from all of the country reading this passage are housed by the University of Wisconsin Digital Collections Center along with all the other fieldwork recordings. They're accessible at digital.library.wisc.edu/1711.dl/AmerLangs.

The six volumes of *DARE* were published between 1985 and 2013. After that, until its funding was cut in 2017,[12] *DARE*'s editorial staff published quarterly updates online and digitally altered segments of the fieldwork recordings to mask information that would give the identity of each informant away.

To see an example of a DARE entry, go to dare.wisc.edu/words/100-entries/kitty-corner. This page defines the term *kitty-corner*, and shows dozens of citations of people who used the term *kitty-corner* and its variants like *kitty-cornered.* Following these citations, *DARE*'s distribution map indicates that *kitty-corner* is commonly distributed in the northern and western parts of the United States and is less common in the southern region.

American Voices, edited by Walt Wolfram and Ben Ward, describes many of the social, ethnic, and regional dialects spoken in the United States. *English Accents & Dialects*, edited by Arthur Hughes, Peter Trudgill, and Dominic Watt, does the same for the United Kingdom and Ireland.

7.4.2 Surveying dialect variation online

Dialect atlases and regional dictionaries are excellent sources that document how language varies. The extremely laborious work of going into remote towns over a wide expanse has been simplified in the modern era as much more evidence can be obtained online. Researchers analyze acoustic data to distinguish the actual qualities of vowel sounds, for example, comparing the 'o' in *stock* as spoken in Chicago versus Boston or Manchester or Glasgow. Phonetic transcriptions that used to be done by ear and laborious computations that used to be done by hand are now quickly done by computer, so a great deal of data can be crunched in a relatively short period of time.

In the early 2000s, Bert Vaux and Scott Golder conducted the Harvard Dialect Survey by means of online surveys. The results of this survey are housed at dialect.redlog.net. There, click "Maps & Results," and you see a list of items that were surveyed, such as the pronunciation of *caramel*. The map associated with that page shows the distribution of where the pronunciation of *caramel* with two syllables and of three syllables predominates. Later, the graphic designer and statistician Joshua Katz represented Vaux and Golder's data in a series of heat maps for the "The Abstract," a North Carolina State University research blog. Many of these maps were later published in Katz's book *Speaking American.*

Bert Vaux has gone on to survey areas outside of the United States, and in many cases, global comparisons can be made. You can view his work at tekstlab.uio.no/cambridge_survey/maps.

7.5 Awareness of biases

With greater awareness than ever of the rich linguistic diversity of human languages, linguists and researchers are attempting to document living languages that are in danger of becoming extinct. In many cases, these languages are structurally different from the languages that most researchers speak.

Often linguists can have biases that are based on familiarity with their own language. Even if you know several languages, if those languages all belong to the same family, you might not consider how other languages are structured. For this reason, many European and American linguistics departments require students to study at least one non-Indo-European language.

Here's an example of a linguistic phenomenon that most speakers of Indo-European languages are not aware of. In *Space in Language and Cognition*, Stephen Levinson describes how in most Indo-European languages, there are different ways to describe the position of an object in space. His example, *The cat is behind the truck*, has two different interpretations:

- The cat is located past the rear end of the truck.
- The truck is located between the speaker and the cat. (That is the cat could be to the left of the truck if the speaker is to the right of the truck.)

A speaker of English processes these interpretations in different areas of the brain. There are languages in which the first interpretation is possible, but the second is not.

The first interpretation is ALLOCENTRIC. That is, the frame of reference takes in the totality of the environment. Such languages usually express location with reference to points of the compass. When a speaker of such a language gestures when retelling a story to indicate, for example, the direction from which an animal is approaching, that gesture will depend on the direction the speaker faces. If the speaker were facing north when the animal approached from the east, they will point to the left (indicating east) when retelling the story only if they are facing north when telling the story. If they are facing south when telling the story, they will point to the right (again, indicating east).

Their frame of reference is through an absolute position, and such languages often do not have words that translate directly as *right* and *left*.

The second interpretation is EGOCENTRIC. That is, the frame of reference is that of the viewpoint of the speaker. This feature is found in all Indo-European languages. If a researcher who speaks an Indo-European language does field work with a population whose language is allocentric, an assumption that egocentric frames of reference were a natural part of all languages would adversely affect the research.

As mentioned in section 6.6, politeness norms vary from culture to culture. Pragmatic differences in cross-cultural or cross-linguistic interactions are a source of many misunderstandings. Before a researcher engages in field work, they must learn about different language structures and conceptualizations so that they don't impose their own linguistic biases on their observations.

7.6 Academic societies

In 1889, the American Dialect Society (ADS) was founded. Dialectology is an important (but not the only) focus of the ADS. Each year since 1991, the ADS has conducted a public meeting during the annual conference, at which their "word of the year" is selected. In 1897, the Yorkshire Dialect Society was founded. It's the oldest dialect society still in existence in the United Kingdom.

Something you can do!

- Go to the websites of the ADS (americandialect.org) and the Yorkshire Dialect Society (yorkshiredialectsociety.org.uk).
- What do these two societies have in common?
- How are these societies different?
- On the ADS site, click on the link to the Word of the Year (americandialect.org/woty) and look at some of the previous nominees and winners. What are some words from the past 12 months that you would nominate at the next meeting? Discuss your choices with your classmates.

The results of research in dialectology and variation are often presented at national or regional meetings of the ADS and the Linguistic Society of America (LSA). At a recent ADS conference, presentations ranged from topics as broad as "Vowels" to one as narrowly focused as an in-depth look at vowel merging in a rural county in southeastern Washington state. If your educational institution has access to Project MUSE, you can access a wealth of original research in their respective publications, *American Speech* (muse.jhu.edu/journal/16) and *Language* (muse.jhu.edu/journal/112).

New Ways of Analyzing Variation (NWAV) is an annual sociolinguistics conference. (There is no central website for this organization. Information about each individual conference can be found on the website of the university that sponsors it.) Papers presented at NWAV deal with language change, language variation, and the way society and culture shape language.

The Society for Pidgin and Creole Linguistics (SPCL) meets annually in conjunction with the LSA. Its publication, *The Journal of Pidgin and Creole Languages*, is available through John Benjamins (jbe-platform.com/content/journals/15699870).

If you're interested in any of the topics in this chapter, you will find these societies to be great resources.

7.7 Conclusion

In this chapter, we've looked at the influence of society and culture on language.[13] We've examined the distinction between language and dialect/variety, and discussed the ways that dialects have been cataloged and recorded. We've looked at the way language changes when two or more languages come into contact, including the role of pidgins and creoles. In the next chapter, we'll discuss usage and style.

7.8 Questions for discussion

• Describe the difference between languages and dialects.
• Describe the difference between pidgins and creoles.

- What are some the different dialect regions of the United States or the United Kingdom? Can you identify some of the differences that distinguish one region from another?
- What kind of information can be found in a dialect atlas?

Notes

1 Further Reading: Milly Jenkins, "Trainspotting – Made Easy for Americans."
2 Further Reading: Lori A. Whynot, *Understanding International Sign*.
3 Further Reading: Mark Sebba, *Contact Languages: Pidgins and Creoles*; Silvia Kouwenberg and John Victor Singler (editors), *The Handbook of Pidgin and Creole Studies*.
4 Further Reading: John Rickford, "The Creole Origins Hypothesis"; Shana Poplack and Sali Tagliamonte, *African American English in the Diaspora*; Walt Wolfram and Erik R. Thomas, *The Development of African American English*.
5 Further Reading: Naomi Wolf, "Young Women, Give Up the Vocal Fry and Reclaim Your Strong Female Voice."
6 Further Reading: The full transcript of this interview is at https://npr.org/templates/transcript/transcript.php?storyId=425608745
7 Further Reading: Erwan Pépiot, "Voice, Speech and Gender: Male-Female Acoustic Differences and Cross-Language Variation in English and French Speakers."
8 Further Reading: Reneé van Bezooijen, "Sociocultural Aspects of Pitch Differences between Japanese and Dutch Women."
9 Further Reading: William Labov, *The Social Stratification of English in New York City*.
10 Further Reading: William Kretzschmar, "Following Kurath: An Appreciation."
11 http://dare.wisc.edu/about/what-is-DARE has information on *DARE*'s methodology.
12 Further Reading: Jesse Sheidlower, "The Closing of a Great American Dialect Project" (online access at https://newyorker.com/culture/cultural-comment/the-closing-of-a-great-american-dialect-project).
13 Further Reading: Carmen Llamas, Louise Mullany, and Peter Stockwell, *The Routledge Companion to Sociolinguistics*.

Chapter 8

Rules, usage, and style

8.0 Introduction

So far, we've explored the natural phenomena associated with language: how people make sounds, arrange these sounds into words that have meaning, arrange these meaningful words into meaningful sequences, and order these meaningful sequences in discourse to communicate ideas.

In this chapter, we explore the rules of language. In school you've likely heard instructors talk about the rules of language, good grammar, proper speech, and the like. But what constitutes a rule?

Not all rules are alike. We'll be looking at three categories of rules:

- *Native rules*: Linguistic rules that native users of a language know without being explicitly taught.
- *Dictated rules*: Rules formulated to represent what is good/bad or right/wrong. These rules are generally taught in English or language arts classes. (Some of the rules of this category that a child's parent or caregiver uses might not have to be explicitly taught to that child.)
- *Guidelines for better communication*: These rules are style guidelines that allow you to express yourself clearly and coherently. They make it easier for your audience to understand you. These rules are also taught.

As we've discussed, *rule* as used in the first and second points represents two different applications of that term. For the third point, I've used the term *guidelines* rather than *rules*. If you violate a guideline, you still might make a well-formed grammatical sentence, but you might not be as understood as clearly as you could be. Also, there's a gray area between the second and third categories. What one person considers to be a dictated rule, another might consider a guideline for better communication. Few language critics categorize rules and guidelines in the exact same way.

In order to discuss rules and guidelines, we will also need to address the topics of usage and style. Most dictionaries provide usage advice, and there are even more usage books than there are dictionaries – not to mention dozens of important style guides. Some guides are geared toward professional editors, others toward writers, and still others for a general audience or for students.

Let's look at these categories individually.

8.1 Native rules

In earlier chapters, we've examined several categories of linguistic rules. For example:

- *Phonological* – Certain speech sounds exist in some languages and not others.

  In English, the consonant cluster [gb] isn't used. (However, this cluster *is* used in other languages, such as those of the Gbe family, which are spoken in a region along the Atlantic coast of Africa from eastern Ghana to western Nigeria). In English, the consonant [ŋ] and the cluster [rd] appear only in the coda of syllables, never the onset. Some languages, like Hawaiian, have fewer clusters; some languages, like Abkhaz, have more.
- *Syntactic* – Some word orders are acceptable in some languages and not others.

  In English, *the the mat cat on is* is not a well-formed sentence. Determiners (like *the*) precede the noun they're associated with ("the dog," not "dog the"). Some languages have a freer word order. As noted in section 6.6, "The woman gave the cat the fish" could be rendered in Czech as *Žena dala kočce rybu*, *Rybu kočce dala žena*, or any other order, because the inflected nouns let you know the grammatical role of each word.

- *Morphological* – In some languages, the adjectives associated with nouns must agree in grammatical gender.

    In Spanish, if you want to use an adjective to describe *una ventana* ("a window"), it has to have the same form as the noun: *una ventana abierta* ("an open window") and not *una ventana abierto*.

Speakers acquire these kinds of rules at a young age. They do not need to be explicitly taught. Young children learn them by listening and interacting with their families and caregivers.[1]

Native speakers generally don't break such rules when speaking. When these rules *are* broken, it's an example of a SPEECH ERROR. (In section 2.4.3 we discussed spoonerisms, which are examples of phonological speech errors, like *heft lemisphere* for *left hemisphere* and *a whole blox of flowers* for *a whole box of flowers.*)[2]

If you learn a language after childhood, you *will* likely have to be taught these kinds of rules. In English, adjectives and nouns don't have grammatical gender, so when English speakers learn a language that has grammatical gender, like German or Spanish, they must learn the rule that the ending of the adjective must agree with the gender of the noun.

On the other hand, the other two categories of rules *are* taught to native speakers of a language.

8.2 Dictated rules

The dictated rules enforce a specific style or elevate one variety of speech over others. They're presented as a "better" way of speaking or writing, or are positioned as the variety of language that you have to learn into order to succeed in school or business.

Dictated rules are taught to enforce a standard, although the concept of "standard" is fuzzy. In the United States and Canada, there isn't an official standard for speaking and writing English. English-speaking countries don't have language academies that stipulate official

English rules in the way the *Académie française* in France does. Nonetheless, centuries of public and private education have resulted in what amounts to a list of rules considered to be the rules of "good grammar."

As far as "proper" speech goes, in England, BBC ENGLISH is the speech used by newscasters at the British Broadcasting Company. It's also referred to as THE QUEEN'S ENGLISH (or, when the ruling monarch is a man, THE KING'S ENGLISH) or RECEIVED PRONUNCIATION. In the United States, there is a generally held perception that there's a generic, "neutral" accent that broadcasters use when speaking.

Many grammar rules taught as the "correct" way of speaking and writing are passed down by tradition in schools. People who don't follow these traditional rules are often stigmatized in society. Speakers of the prestigious varieties of English may consider speakers who don't follow these rules to be uneducated or from a lower socioeconomic class. Students or adults who aren't well versed in the traditional rules will often be advised to learn, or feel compelled to learn, these rules in order to accrue the benefits, such as access to better jobs, that are associated with speakers of a prestigious variety.

Something you can do!

- Name five rules of English that you've been taught in school.
- In what contexts do you follow or ignore these rules?

The following sections outline some rules you were probably taught in school to differentiate "good" or "proper" English from "bad" or "improper" English.

8.2.1 Examples of dictated phonological rules

- "Don't drop the – g in words like *running* or *fishing*."

In describing this phonological phenomenon, people usually conflate spelling with sound. The written sequence 'ng' doesn't stand for the sound [n] followed by the sound [g]. Rather, 'ng' stands for the velar nasal sound [ŋ]. (The phonology of nasal consonants is covered in section 2.2.1.2.) So, when people say *eatin'* instead of *eating*, they are uttering [itɪn] instead of [itɪŋ]. No sound has been dropped. Instead, the velar nasal [ŋ] has been replaced with alveolar nasal [n].

The contexts where [ŋ] changes to [n] aren't universal. Someone who pronounces *eating* as [itɪn] will still pronounce *bring* as [brɪŋ] (and not [brɪn]) and *lung* as [lʊŋ] (not [lʊn]). The context where this velar to alveolar change occurs is in the present participle suffix *–ing*. As such, it is a well-formed pattern: speakers who replace [ŋ] with [n] apply it only in the relevant contexts, not willy-nilly. It is a legitimate phonological variation found in several different varieties of English. Speakers of those varieties who decide to speak what they view as a more prestigious variety of English have to learn to articulate [ŋ] instead of [n] in the appropriate contexts.

- "Don't drop the first *r* in *library* or *February*."

    Often these words are pronounced as "libary" and "Febuary." The more rapidly you speak, the more likely you are to drop certain sounds. You can articulate every sound in a sentence like "Where did you go last night?" if you speak slowly. Spoken rapidly, "Where did you" can come out as "wairdja." Outside of diction classes, this type of phonological elision is usually unremarkable, but the loss of certain consonants, like the first *r* in *library* or *February*, is often taken as a sign of shoddy language skills or ignorance. It's arbitrary that these two words have been chosen as a test that separates proper speech from improper speech.

- "The word *ask* is pronounced [æsk] – not [æks], as though it were written *ax* or *aks*."

    Section 2.4.3 discussed metathesis, the phenomenon where two sounds or syllables are transposed within a word. It's a common process by which words in a language change over time: *third* was *thridde* in Middle English, and *bird* was *brid* in Old

English. Although the pronunciation of *ask* as *ax* is often considered to be a stigmatized feature of some varieties of English, including African American English, both the [ks] and [sk] forms were used in the Old English and Middle English equivalents of the word without stigma.[3]

Something you can do!

- Write down a list of words that teachers, parents, or other authority figures have told you that you pronounce differently from what is considered the standard pronunciation.
- In what social contexts do you use these pronunciations? In what social contexts, if any, would you use the standard form?
- Write down a list of words that you have heard other people pronounce in a way that is considered nonstandard. (Keep in mind that some words, like *almond* or *harass*, have multiple standard pronunciations.) What reaction do you have when others use those forms instead of the forms that are considered standard?

8.2.2 Examples of dictated morphological and syntactic rules

- "*Seen* is the past participle and not the simple past tense of *saw*. *I seen it* is properly rendered as *I saw it* or *I had seen it*."
- "*Ain't* is a nonstandard contraction."[4]
- "In conjoined phrases, always put *I* or *me* in the second position and use nominative forms in the subject position. The standard rule dictates the construction *He and I went to the beach* (not *Me and him went to the beach* or *I and he went to the beach*)."
- "Objective pronouns should be used as objects of verbs and prepositions: *Sheila gave him and me the box* is correct (not *Sheila gave he and I the box*). *The song was sung by Cammie and me* is correct (not *The song was sung by Cammie and I*)."

8.2.3 Examples of dictated rules regarding word choice

- "*Lie* is used as an intransitive verb: it doesn't take an object. (*The baby lies in the crib.*) Its past-tense form is *lay*: *The baby lay in the crib.* Its past participle form is *lain*: *The baby had lain in the crib for 20 minutes before falling asleep.*"
- "*Lay* is used as a transitive verb: it takes an object. (*I lay the baby in the crib and then turn out the light.*) Its past tense and past participle form is *laid*: *I laid the baby in the crib. After I had laid the baby in the crib, I sang softly until he fell asleep.*"
- "*Fewer* should be used with things that you can count: *This line is for people with fewer than 12 items. Less* should be used with mass nouns: *There is less gas in the car than there was yesterday.*"
- Sometimes people claim that nonstandard words, like *ain't* and *irregardless*,[5] aren't actually words. Both of these examples are included in most major dictionaries, and even though they are traditionally categorized as nonstandard, they are nonetheless words. Even though it is highly stigmatized, the use of *ain't* is a feature in many varieties of English.

8.2.4 Examples of dictated spelling rules

Spelling rules are dictated, but they're different than dictated rules of speech.

All spelling rules are arbitrary. As we'll discuss in Section 8.4, spelling in Middle English was inconsistent. As literacy rates improved, there was a move toward consistency. Early Modern English lexicographers like Samuel Johnson helped to make spelling consistent.

Dictated phonological, morphological, and syntactic rules for speech aren't always in accordance with how people actually speak. In some varieties of English, [ŋ] is replaced with [n] in some contexts. Young children learn to speak the language in which they are spoken to.

On the other hand, everyone is instructed how to spell. Replacing [ŋ] with [n] isn't arbitrary. Spelling *cat* as c-a-t is arbitrary. As such, even though English orthography is very inconsistent, especially when compared to many other languages, there are standard ways of spelling words, leading to rules like:

- "*All right* is never spelled *alright* (despite the existence of pairs like *all ready/already*)."
- "*A lot* is never spelled *alot*."
- "*Stationery* refers to paper that you write letters on, and *stationary* is an adjective for describing things that remain in place."

8.2.5 Changes and shifts in dictated rules

Dictated rules are frequently seen as gatekeepers that separate "good" English from "bad" English. But what's considered to be an indication of "broken" or "improper" English changes over time.

Sometimes a person doesn't even realize when they've encountered a rule violation. For example, purists would state that singular subjects like *a person* must take singular pronouns like *he* or *she* or *one* and not *they*, without having realized that *they* has for centuries been analyzed as a singular pronoun. You might not have noticed that throught this book (including the first sentence in this paragraph) singular *they* has been used – that's how entrenched the use of singular *they* is in the language.

In recent decades a push has been made to recognize that this is simply how language is used and that this fact should be reflected in the standard language. Even style guides like the *Associated Press Stylebook* now acknowledge that using singular *they* is acceptable, and so do many dictionaries.[6]

Other times, the arbitrariness of a rule is called into question and a formerly cut-and-dried rule is no longer strongly enforced.

For example, in the 1800s, some grammarians decided that English should operate like Latin. English is a Germanic language (like Dutch and German), and Latin is a Romance language (like Spanish and French). They imposed and promulgated certain restrictions on English to make it more like Latin. For example, they warned against:

- *Splitting infinitives.* This rule would prevent you from placing words between *to* and the following verb in infinitive phrases. So, for example, "to boldly go" – as used in the opening of *Star Trek* – is a violation of this rule. In Latin, the infinitive is represented by a single word and therefore cannot be split: the English infinitive phrase "to go" is *ire* in Latin. But there's no good reason why this rule should apply to English. Following this rule creates clunky sentences that sound odd. Linguists have long called into question the need for this rule, and you're likely to encounter it only highly formal contexts or from writers who feel compelled to follow this arbitrary, useless rule.[7]
- *Ending sentences with prepositions.* Latin is a highly inflected language, and many prepositional phrases in English are rendered in Latin as a single inflected word. However, forcing this rule in English creates stilted sentences. You probably haven't even noticed that this book has been written avoiding this rule. For example, in the previous section, I wrote "*Stationery* refers to paper that you write letters on" and not "*Stationery* refers to paper on which you write letters."

Some rules change or drop out over time, and others stay in effect. Although more reference works and style guides have softened the stance against singular *they*, split infinitives, and ending sentences with prepositions, certain prohibitions live on.

It's likely that *ain't* will always be considered nonstandard, because most language teachers insist that it is an incorrect form. The use of *ain't*, however, follows perfectly logical syntactic formations and is a feature of several varieties of English. Many people claim *irregardless* is not a word. People who bristle against *irregardless* ignore the fact that its relationship to *regardless* is analogous to similarly structured, unremarkable pairs like *unravel/ravel* and *debone/bone*.

In the introductory chapter, I mentioned that using *contact* as a verb (as in *When you're ready to submit a proposal, please contact my office*) was once considered incorrect. How can something that seems so completely correct to a present-day speaker have been considered such an egregious error? Like many English verbs, *contact* started out as a noun. During the transition period when people began using *contact* as a verb, there was great resistance to this usage. The conclusion of the *American Heritage Dictionary* usage note at *contact* reads: "In 1969, only 34 percent of the Usage Panel accepted the use of *contact* as a verb, but in 1988, 65 percent of the Panel accepted it in the sentence *She immediately called an officer at the Naval Intelligence Service, who in turn contacted the FBI.* In 2004, fully 94 percent accepted *contact* in this same sentence." That's a remarkable change in judgment over a relatively brief period of time.

Preferred pronunciations also change over time. In addition to the pronunciation of *harass*, which is discussed in section 2.5, examples include the pronunciation of *forte* as FOR-tay (the older pronunciation is FORT), the pronunciation of *zoology* as ZOO-ol-uh-jee (the older pronunciation is ZOE-ol-uh-jee), and the pronunciation of *xenophobia* as ZEE-nuh-foe-be-uh (the older pronunciation is ZEN-uh-foe-be-uh).

Standardized spelling rules change, too. In the 1800s, the American lexicographer Noah Webster made several systematic spelling changes. For example, Webster dropped the 'u' in words like *labour* and *honour*. Those are still the standard spellings in the United Kingdom, Canada, and other past and current members of the British Commonwealth, but in the United States, they're spelled *labor* and *honor*.

Since dictated rules are arbitrary, they can and do change. Sometimes the change itself is arbitrary, and sometimes it is because the dictated rules don't conform to or clash with native rules. Change to native rules can also occur due to factors like the upheaval associated with language contact (as when the Norman French conquered England in 1066, or when European colonialists overtook indigenous populations and brought enslaved people from other places).

8.3 Guidelines for better communication

These kinds of rules are usually not presented as "right" or "wrong." Instead, they're usually associated with writing instead of speech and are often couched as helpful advice to make your writing crisper. They help you communicate more effectively.

Here are examples of guidelines grouped by category:

- "Be concise."

    Your communication is simpler and easier to comprehend if you use simple phrases or single words in place of longer phrases. For example:

Instead of	Use
at such time as	when
in the event that	if
should you require any assistance	if you need help
please don't hesitate to ask	please ask

    Nothing is grammatically incorrect about the sentence *At such time as you are in the process of relocating, please don't hesitate to call if you need assistance.* However, *When you're relocating, please call if you need help* conveys the same message more straightforwardly. In publishing and communications companies, copyeditors are responsible for making written passages more readable.

- "Be clear."

    Clear speech is easier to understand. For example, avoid clustering nouns in awkward phrases like *traffic accident prevention committee policies.* Instead, consider using prepositional phrases, like *the policies of the committee to prevent traffic accidents.* Keep your audience in mind and use language they will readily comprehend. As mentioned in Chapter 5, because many people think *inflammable* means "not flammable" (when in fact, it means "flammable"), it might be preferable to use phrases like *likely to catch on fire.* A statement like *The water is not potable* is more clearly expressed as *This water is not meant for drinking* or *It is not safe to drink this water.*

- "Use parallel constructions."

    When items are joined by conjunctions, it's easier to understand if the phrases on both sides have the same syntactic construction. Even though *to go to the museum* and *pizza* are both possible arguments of the verb *want*, a sentence like *Shannon wanted to go to the museum and pizza* is more clearly expressed as *Shannon wanted to go to the museum and to eat pizza*.

• "Avoid sexist language."

In recent years, many style guides have given the thumbs up to singular *they*, so that instead of saying *Everyone took his hat and left*, you can say *Everyone took their hat and left*. However, even if you don't use (or are not allowed to use) singular *they*, you can still recast the sentence to avoid the sexist use of masculine pronouns to refer to men and women or to unknown referents: *All the people took their hats and left*. Avoiding sexist language includes using words and phrases like *humankind*, *synthetic*, and *staffing the table* instead of *mankind*, *manmade*, and *manning the table*.

Some stylebooks refer to these suggestions as rules. But these rules are of a different kind than dictated rules. If you violate dictated rules, you might be judged as not knowing how to speak or write correctly, depending on your audience. If you mix up the distinction between *lie* and *lay*, people will still understand what you're saying. *Lie the book down on the table* is considered a grammatical error, but if you said it, your audience would still understand what you're saying.

On the other hand, if you violate guidelines for better communication, there's a different effect. You could lose your audience's attention, confuse them, lead them to faulty conclusions, or offend them. Miscommunication could lead to misunderstanding.

There are several kinds of style guides. Most don't address topics involving native rules. English style guides written for speakers of English do not need to spell out that *the* and *a* come before a noun and not after. (Reference works that are directed toward adult learners of a language will include much more on native rules, of course.) Rather, most style guides explore pitfalls that keep you from communicating effectively and offer solutions to these problems.

Among authors of style guides, there's a wide range of opinion as to where to place the line between dictated rules that you can choose to follow or ignore and style rules that improve communication. In *A Sense of Style*, Steven Pinker encourages us to split infinitives and forget about the distinction between *convince* and *persuade*; on the other hand, he also reminds us the importance of knowing that *credible* means "believable" and not "credulous" and that *enervate* means "weaken" and not "energize." Strunk and White's *The Elements of Style* and Bryan Garner's *Garner's Modern English Usage* follow more traditional approaches and encourage readers to follow dictated rules. Garner uses a five-point "language-change index" that indicates the degree to which a change in traditional usage is rejected or accepted.[8]

Some guides focus on a specific topic. The book *Eats, Shoots & Leaves* by Lynne Truss deals solely with punctuation. The focus of the blog *Conscious Style Guide*, edited by Karen Yin, is inclusive, respectful language regarding ability and disability; age; gender, sex, and sexuality; ethnicity, race, and nationality; and similar topics.

Other well-known style guides include Claire Kehrwald Cook's *Line by Line*, the *Chicago Manual of Style* (now in its seventeenth edition), and the *Associated Press Stylebook* (apstylebook.com). Many universities have online resources devoted to issues of style, such as the Purdue Online Writing Lab (owl.english.purdue.edu/owl). ACES: The Society for Editing (aceseditors.org) also provides excellent resources.

8.4 Rules: clarity and consistency versus power

Historically, arbitrary norms have been established through a combination of the desire for clarity and consistency and the desire for power.

The Middle English period was from about 1100 to 1500. Most entries in the *Middle English Dictionary* include numerous variants found in the writings of that period. The printing press was invented in the mid-1400s. Written documents became more accessible, and more people learned to read. With the rise of literacy came conformity. Rudimentary word lists and glossaries helped establish spelling norms, enabling the further spread of literacy.

Style guides create consistency. Very large organizations need consistency when they communicate with their audiences. As a noun, is it *health-care, health care*, or *healthcare*? You'll find evidence for all of these styles, but within a publishing organization, usually one style is preferred. Reporters and copyeditors who work for news organizations that are members of the Associated Press (AP) will follow AP style, as outlined in the *Associated Press Stylebook*. For spelling words and determining whether a word like *health-care* is hyphenated, an open compound, or a solid word, the AP relies on *Webster's New World College Dictionary*. In the isolated instances where the AP favors a different form, the difference is indicated in the *AP Stylebook*. The existence of the *AP Stylebook* results in a consistent style across many organizations.

Many major newspapers, like the *New York Times* and the *London Times*, have internal style guides that stipulate whether their editors can use singular *they* or spell *co-worker* without a hyphen. Formerly, most newspapers' style rules were strongly enforced. As newspaper staffs have gotten smaller, several editorial layers have been stripped away, and nowadays you'll see more inconsistencies in style than before 2010. And as news hits the internet the moment it happens, often writers have to edit their own work. Mistakes frequently crop up, possibly only to be edited when someone in the comments section points out a misspelling.

On the flip side of clarity and conformity, throughout human history, the people in control have clashed with the powerless. One way the powerful have tried consolidating power is by limiting the others' ability to take their power away. Language can be suppressed by legislation and other political means, through the institution of social hierarchies that maintain the status quo, and by brute force. Language has long been used as a weapon to separate the haves from the have-nots and the educated from the uneducated. By maintaining that a set of rules must be observed in order to gain access to good jobs, good schools, and opportunities to make money, it's easy to maintain this separation.

From a linguistic point of view, each variety of a language is as valid a form of communication as any other variety. For educators, there's value in helping students achieve success by teaching them an accepted standard variety, and this education can take place without demeaning or denigrating other varieties. Language isn't a static monolith consisting of ossified rules. English, like all living languages, changes as people use it. Change is inevitable, and we should celebrate and respect the diversity of English.

8.5 Conclusion

In this chapter, we've examined the different kinds of rules associated with language. We've looked at the natural rules that children learn as native speakers of a language and the arbitrary rules that are imposed onto language, whether for conformity, clarity, or adherence to a standard. We've explored what it means to have the viewpoint that all varieties of language are valid forms of communication.

The next chapter, the final chapter, is a summary of the topics that have been covered in this book.

8.6 Questions for discussion

- What is the distinction between native and arbitrary rules?
- What are some reasons that arbitrary rules exist?
- From a linguistic standpoint, how do speech and writing that conform to the rules of a standard variety differ from speech and writing that do not?
- How does the fact that language changes affect the way you view language rules?

Notes

1 Further Reading: Jerome Bruner, *Child's Talk*; Eve Clark, *First Language Acquisition*.
2 Further Reading: Victoria Fromkin (editor), *Speech Errors as Linguistic Evidence*. The examples shown here are from the appendix, pages 243–269.
3 Further Reading: The *Our Living Language* essay at the entry for **ax** in the *American Heritage Dictionary* (online access at https://ahdictionary.com/word/search.html?q=ax).
4 Further Reading: The usage note at the entry for **ain't** in the *Merriam-Webster Collegiate Dictionary* (online access at https://merriam-webster.com/dictionary/ain't).
5 Further Reading: Kory Stamper, *Word by Word*, the chapter "Irregardless: On Wrong Words."

6 Further Reading: Merrill Perlman, "Will 'They' Ever Change?" (online access at https://cjr.org/language_corner/will_they_ever_change.php).
7 Further Reading: The usage note at the entry for **split infinitive** at Dictionary.com (online access at www.dictionary.com/browse/split-infinitive).
8 Further Reading: Tom Freeman, "Bryan Garner's Language Change Index" (online access at https://stroppyeditor.wordpress.com/2014/05/14/bryan-garners-language-change-index/).

Chapter 9

Conclusion

9.0 Introduction

This chapter summarizes the topics covered in this book. It also provides information about additional linguistic subfields, career possibilities that involve or are enhanced by the study of linguistics, and linguistics organizations in the United States, the United Kingdom, and Canada.

I hope you've found the material engaging. If you have, I encourage you to enroll in other classes and read related books about subjects you've found interesting.

9.1 Chapter-by-chapter summary

Chapter 1 provided a *general overview*. You were asked to think critically about language and language change. We compared and contrasted written material from Old English, Middle English, and early Modern English, examining similarities and differences across the centuries.

Chapter 2 dealt with *phonology* and *phonetics*. You learned about sound production in the human vocal tract. We discussed how these sounds are categorized and how they can be combined. We also looked at changes in sound over time.

Chapter 3 dealt with *morphology*. You learned that words have base forms and how adding derivational or inflectional morphemes alters their meaning. We discussed how morphemes can combine in a language and discussed morphological change over time.

Chapter 4 dealt with *syntax*. You learned about the parts of speech and their roles in forming a sentence. We discussed how words combine to form sentences in English and how English syntax changes over time.

Chapter 5 dealt with *semantics* and *lexical semantics*. You learned about the concept of meaning, how the meanings of words change over time, and how new meanings arise. We discussed how philosophers and linguists have analyzed how thoughts are communicated through language.

Chapter 6 dealt with *pragmatics*. You learned how context and conventional maxims of conversation allow users of language to convey more than the straightforward meaning of the words used. We discussed the concepts of reference and politeness.

Chapter 7 dealt with *sociolinguistics* and *language variation*. You learned how social factors have a role in how speech communities use language. We also discussed how a language can vary from place to place and ways that these changes and differences are documented.

Chapter 8 dealt with *usage*. Earlier chapters focused on natural phenomena of language; this chapter looked into stylistic rules and guidelines. We discussed the role of dictionaries and style guides.

These chapters constitute a simple overview of these linguistic areas of study, especially with respect to English and language change in English. At most universities, linguistics departments and many English departments offer classes that focus on these topics individually.

9.2 Other fields of study in linguistics

In addition to the primary areas of linguistic study we've examined, there are many subfields within these categories that might interest you. Here are just a few, along with sources for more information. Many of these books can be found in your institution's library. (Full bibliographical information is in the References section following this chapter.)

Child language acquisition examines how children come to understand and produce language by interacting with caregivers and other adults and children, including the production of single-word utterances, how they string words together into longer phrases, the kinds of errors that they make in the process of learning, and how they learn about exceptions to observed patterns.

Further reading

Jerome Bruner, *Child's Talk: Learning to Use Language*
Eve Clark, *Language in Children*
Caroline Rowland, *Understanding Child Language Acquisition*

Computational linguistics involves computational models of natural language. Topics within this field include machine translation, speech recognition, speech synthesis, text and data mining, computer-mediated language learning, and *natural language processing*, which has to do with programming computers to analyze and obtain meaning from human language.

Further reading

Alexander Clark, Chris Fox, and Shalom Lappin (editors), *The Handbook of Computational Linguistics and Natural Language Processing*
Ruslan Mitkov (editor), *The Oxford Handbook of Computational Linguistics*

Contact linguistics is the study of language contact (as mentioned in Chapter 7). This is a subfield within sociolinguistics that examines the different ways languages influence each other when speakers of different languages interact.

Further reading

Yaron Matras, *Language Contact*
Sarah Thomason, *Language Contact: An Introduction*
Donald Winford, *An Introduction to Contact Linguistics*

Forensic linguistics involves the application of linguistic field methods to establish facts or evidence in a court of law or otherwise aid in criminal investigations. Forensic linguists testify to what is meant by a defendant's speech or writing. Outside of the courtroom, their skills can be used in surveillance and to aid government agencies in collecting intelligence.

Further reading

Judith Levy, "Language as Evidence: The Linguist as Expert Witness in North American Courts"

Malcolm Coulthard and Alison Johnson (editors), *The Routledge Handbook of Forensic Linguistics*

Historical linguistics is the study of the change of language over time. Some historical linguists describe and categorize the changes. Others explain how or why these changes occurred. Many of the examples of change in language that you have learned about in this textbook fall under the category of historical linguistics.

Further reading

Claire Bowern and Bethwyn Evans (editors), *The Routledge Handbook of Historical Linguistics*

April M. S. McMahon, *Understanding Language Change*

Robert McColl Millar and Larry Trask, *Trask's Historical Linguistics*, third edition

Linguistic anthropology examines the ways language affects and shapes culture. As the name implies, it's an interdisciplinary field, involving both linguistics and anthropology.

Further reading

Harriet Joseph Ottenheimer, *The Anthropology of Language*

Bambi Schieffelin, Kathryn A. Woolard, and Paul V. Kroskrity (editors), *Language Ideologies: Practice and Theory*

Phonetic acoustics is the study of the acoustic properties of the sounds of speech. Topics in this field include the production of sound waves, the properties of these waves, and the way sound waves interact with anatomical features in your ear and are perceived by the brain as sound. Plotting the frequencies of the components that make up speech sounds allows researchers to analyze speech production and track phonological change over time in speech communities.

Further reading

Ian MacKay, *Phonetics: The Science of Speech Production*, second edition
Kenneth N. Stevens, *Acoustic Phonetics*

Psycholinguistics involves the psychological and biological processes within the brain that give rise to the acquisition and use of language. Psycholinguists examine the role of the brain in language comprehension and production.

Further reading

Lise Menn and Nina F. Dronkers, *Psycholinguistics: Introduction and Applications*, second edition
Steven Pinker, *The Language Instinct*
Matthew J. Traxler, *Introduction to Psycholinguistics*

Typology involves the classification of languages throughout the world in terms of their structural features, showing similarities and differences. Typology examines the common features within languages in the same language families and explains the diversity in language structure across the globe.

Further reading

William Croft, *Typology and Universals*, second edition
Viveka Velupillai, *An Introduction to Linguistic Typology*

9.3 What's next?

You are surrounded by language. You encounter it daily. Language is your connection to the world around you and the people you interact with. Language change is ongoing, and you influence change in language by using it.

Now that you're more familiar with the English language and how English undergoes change, you might be asking yourself, "What can I do with a degree in linguistics?"

Studying linguistics not only provides you with a solid liberal arts education, but it can provide a solid foundation for a career in advertising and branding, artificial intelligence, audiology, cognitive science, copyediting and proofreading, education, information and library science, law, lexicography, literacy programming and instruction, publishing, speech pathology, speech recognition, teaching English as a second language, technical writing, or translation, to name a few.

I hope that this textbook has piqued your curiosity and that you will continue to learn more about how language shapes society and the world we live in. If you've developed an interest in linguistics, talk to your instructor about further courses of study. Many questions about language and how it works remain unexplored. Countless languages and dialects on the verge of extinction have not been cataloged or studied.

Check out the following organizations for more information:

- Linguistic Society of America (linguisticsociety.org), especially the FAQ (linguisticsociety.org/resource/faq)
- American Association of Applied Linguistics (aaal.org)
- Linguistics Association for Great Britain (lagb.org.uk)
- British Association for Applied Linguistics (baal.org.uk)
- Canadian Linguistic Association (cla-acl.ca)
- Canadian Association of Applied Linguistics (aclacaal.org)

With so many disciplines in the field of linguistics, anyone interested in language and language change can pursue academic studies in an area they find compelling, challenging, and exciting.

References

Abbott, Barbara. 2017. "Reference." In *The Oxford Handbook of Pragmatics*, edited by Yan Huang. Pages 240–258. Oxford: Oxford University Press.

Ahrens, Lynn. 1974. "Interjections!" [Television series episode]. In *Schoolhouse Rock*. New York: McCaffrey & McCall/Production Company.

Algeo, John and Carmen A. Butcher. 2014. *The Origins and Development of the English Language*, seventh edition. Boston: Wadsworth Publishing, Cengage Learning.

Allsop, Richard, editor. 1996. *Dictionary of Caribbean English Usage*. Oxford: Oxford University Press.

American Heritage Dictionaries. 2011. *The American Heritage Student Grammar Dictionary*. Boston/New York: Houghton Mifflin Harcourt.

American Heritage Dictionaries. 2018. *The American Heritage Dictionary of the English Language*, fifth edition: 50th anniversary. Boston/New York: Houghton Mifflin Harcourt.

Associated Press. 2017. *Associated Press Stylebook 2017*. New York: The Associated Press.

Austin, John L. 1962. *How to Do Things with Words*. Cambridge, MA: Harvard University Press.

Baker, Peter S. 2012. *Introduction to Old English*, third edition. Malden/Oxford/Chichester: Wiley-Blackwell.

Bilefsky, Dan. 2016. "Period. Full Stop. Point. Whatever It's Called, It's Going Out of Style." *New York Times*. June 10, 2016. Page A1.

Bowern, Claire and Bethwyn Evans, editors. 2012. *The Routledge Handbook of Historical Linguistics*. Abingdon/New York: Routledge.

Brinton, Laurel J. and Leslie K. Arnovick. 2017. *The English Language: A Linguistic History*, third edition. Don Mills: Canada Oxford University Press.

Brown, Penelope and Stephen Levinson. 1978. "Universals in Language Usage: Politeness Phenomena." In *Questions and Politeness: Strategies in Social Interaction*, edited by Esther N. Goody. Pages 56–310. Cambridge: Cambridge University Press.

Brown, Penelope and Stephen Levinson. 1987. *Politeness: Some Universals in Language Usage*. Cambridge: Cambridge University Press.

Bruner, Jerome. 1983. *Child's Talk: Learning to Use Language*. Oxford: Oxford University Press.

Cassidy, Frederic and Joan Houston Hall, editors. 1985–2013. *Dictionary of American Regional English*, volumes 1–6. Cambridge: Harvard University Press.

Chaucer, Geoffrey. 1387–1400. *The Canterbury Tales*. http://librarius.com/cantales.htm

Chaucer, Geoffrey and Jill Mann, editors. 2005. *The Canterbury Tales*. New York: Penguin Classics.

Clark, Alexander, Chris Fox, and Shalom Lappin, editors. 2013. *The Handbook of Computational Linguistics and Natural Language Processing*, first edition. Malden/Oxford/Chichester: Wiley-Blackwell.

Clark, Eve. 2003. *First Language Acquisition*. Cambridge: Cambridge University Press.

Clark, Herbert H. 1992. *Arenas of Language Use*. Chicago: University of Chicago Press/Center for the Study of Language and Information.

Collins, John. 2008. *Chomsky: A Guide for the Perplexed*. London/New York: Continuum International Publishing Group.

Cook, Claire Kehrwald. 1985. *Line by Line: How to Edit Your Own Writing*. Boston: Houghton Mifflin Harcourt.

Coulthard, Malcom and Alison Johnson, editors. 2010. *The Routledge Handbook of Forensic Linguistics*. Abingdon/New York: Routledge.

Croft, William. 2003. *Typology and Universals*, second edition. Cambridge: Cambridge University Press.

Crystal, David. 2014. *Language Death*, second edition. Cambridge: Cambridge University Press.

Dictionary.com. 2017. "Dictionary.com Unabridged." *Split Infinitive*. www.dictionary.com/browse/split-infinitive

Eckert, Penelope. 1989a. *Jocks and Burnouts: Social Categories and Identities in High School*. New York: Teachers College Press.

Eckert, Penelope. 1989b. "The Whole Woman: Sex and Gender Differences in Variation." *Language Variation and Change*. Volume 1, pages 245–268.

Eckert, Penelope. 2015. Interviewed in "From Upspeak to Vocal Fry: Are We 'Policing' Young Women's Voices?" *Fresh Air* (Terry Gross, host), July 23, 2015. Philadelphia: WHYY, National Public Radio. Transcript. https://npr.org/templates/transcript/transcript.php?storyId=425608745

Fey, Tina. 2004. *Mean Girls* [motion picture]. Los Angeles: Paramount Pictures.

Fillmore, Charles. 1968. "The Case for Case." In *Universals in Linguistic Theory*, edited by Emmon Bach and Robert T. Harms. Pages 1–88. New York: Holt, Rinehart, and Winston.

Fillmore, Charles. 1970. "The Grammar of *Hitting* and *Breaking*." In *Readings in English Transformational Grammar*, edited by Roderick Jacobs and Peter Rosenbaum. Pages 120–133. Waltham: Ginn.

Freeman, Tom. 2014. "Bryan Garner's Language-Change Index." *Stroppy Editor* (blog). https://stroppyeditor.wordpress.com/2014/05/14/bryan-garners-language-change-index/

Frege, Gottlob. 1952. "On Sense and Reference." In *Translations from the Philosophical Writings of Gottlob Frege*, edited by Peter T. Geach and Max Black. Pages 56–78. Oxford: Blackwell. Originally published 1892, as "Über Sinn und Bedeutung." In *Zeitschrift für Philosophie und philosophische Kritik*. Volume 100, pages 25–50.

Fromkin, Victoria, editor. 1973. *Speech Errors as Linguistic Evidence*. The Hague, Paris: Mouton.

Garner, Bryan A. 2009. *Garner's Modern American Usage*, third edition. New York: Oxford University Press.

Goffman, Erving. 1963. *Behavior in Public Places: Notes on the Social Organization of Gatherings*. New York: The Free Press.

Green, Lisa J. 2002. *African American English: A Linguistic Introduction*. Cambridge: Cambridge University Press.

Grey, Sarah. 2017. "Salvaging the Dormant: On Language." *Salvage*. Number 5 (October 2017), pp. 95–108. http://salvage.zone/in-print/salvaging-the-dormant-on-language/

Grice, H. Paul. 1975. "Logic and Conversation." In *Syntax & Semantics, Volume 3: Speech Acts*, edited by Peter Cole and Jerry Morgan. New York: Academic Press.

Gummere, Francis, translator. 1910. *Beowulf.* Harvard Classics Series. New York: P. F. Collier & Son.

Hancock, Adrienne and Benjamin Rubin. 2015. "Influence of Communication Partner's Gender on Language." *Journal of Language and Social Psychology.* Volume 34, number 1, pages 46–64.

Haspelmath, Martin and Andrea Sims. 2010. *Understanding Morphology*, second edition. Abingdon/New York: Routledge.

Heaney, Seamus, translator. 2012. *Beowulf: A New Verse Translation.* New York City: Farrar, Straus & Giroux.

Horn, Larry. 1984. "Toward a New Taxonomy for Pragmatic Inference: Q-Based and R-Based Implicature." In *Meaning, Form and Use in Context: Linguistic Applications (GURT)*, edited by Deborah Schiffrin. Washington: Georgetown University Press.

Hughes, Arthur, Peter Trudgill, and Dominic Watt, editors. 2012. *English Accents & Dialects*, fifth edition. London/New York: Routledge.

Jenkins, Millie. 1996. "'Trainspotting' – Made Easy for Americans." *The Independent.* May 25, 1996. www.independent.co.uk/news/uk/home-news/trainspotting-made-easy-for-americans-1349197.html

Jucker, Andreas H. 2017. "Pragmatics and Language Change: Historical Pragmatics." In *The Oxford Handbook of Pragmatics*, edited by Yan Huang. Pages 550–566. Oxford: Oxford University Press.

Kapitan, Alex. 2017. "On 'Person-First Language': It's Time to Actually Put the Person First." *Radical Copy Editor* (blog). July 3, 2017. https://radicalcopyeditor.com/2017/07/03/person-centered-language/

Katz, Joshua. 2016. *Speaking American.* Boston/New York: Houghton Mifflin Harcourt.

Kleinedler, Steve. 2000. "Have Your Salt and Eat It, Too." *Verbatim: The Language Quarterly.* Volume 25, number 1, pages 20–23.

Kleinedler, Steve. 2009. "The Semantics of Marriage Equality." *The Advocate* (blog). www.advocate.com/news/news-features/2009/11/24/semantics-marriage-equality

Kouwenberg, Silvia and John Victor Singler, editors. 2008. *The Handbook of Pidgin and Creole Studies.* Malden/Oxford/Chichester: Wiley-Blackwell.

Kretzschmar, William A., Jr. 2002. "Following Kurath: An Appreciation." *Dictionaries: Journal of the Dictionary Society of North America.* Volume 23, number 1, pages 115–124.

Kurath, Hans, Marcus Hansen, Bernard Bloch, and Julia Bloch. 1939. *Handbook of the Linguistic Geography of New England*. Providence: Brown University Press.

Kurath, Hans and Sherman Kuhn, editors. 1954–2001. *The Middle English Dictionary*. Ann Arbor: University of Michigan Press.

Labov, William. 1966. *The Social Stratification of English in New York City*. Washington: Center for Applied Linguistics.

Labov, William. 1990. "The Intersection of Sex and Social Class in the Course of Linguistic Change." *Language Variation and Change*. Volume 2, number 2, pages 205–254.

Landau, Sidney I. 2001. *Dictionaries: The Art and Craft of Lexicography*, second edition. Cambridge: Cambridge University Press.

Levin, Beth. 1993. *English Verb Classes and Alternations: A Preliminary Investigation*. Chicago: University of Chicago Press.

Levinson, Stephen C. 2000. *Presumptive Meanings*. Cambridge, MA: MIT Press.

Levinson, Stephen C. 2003. *Space in Language and Cognition*. Cambridge, UK: Cambridge University Press.

Levy, Judith. 1994. "Language as Evidence: The Linguist as Expert Witness in North American Courts." *Forensic Linguistics: The International Journal of Speech, Language, and the Law*. Volume 1, number 1, pages 1–26.

Ling, Rich and Naomi S. Baron. 2007. *Text Messaging and IM: Linguistic Comparison of American College Data*. Washington, DC: Department of Language and Foreign Studies, American University.

Llamas, Carmen, Louise Mullany, and Peter Stockwell, editors. 2007. *The Routledge Companion to Sociolinguistics*. Abingdon/New York: Routledge.

Lynch, Jack. 2016. *You Could Look It Up*. New York/London: Bloomsbury Press.

MacKay, Ian R. A. 1987. *Phonetics: The Science of Speech Production*, second edition. Boston/Toronto/San Diego: A College-Hill Production – Little, Brown and Company.

Matras, Yaron. 2009. *Language Contact*. Cambridge: Cambridge University Press.

McCawley, James. 1988. *The Syntactic Phenomena of English*, volume 1. Chicago: University of Chicago Press.

McCawley, James. 1998. *The Syntactic Phenomena of English*, volume 2. Chicago: University of Chicago Press.

McLendon, Lisa. *Madam Grammar* (blog). https://madamgrammar.com

McMahon, April M. S. 1994. *Understanding Language Change*. Cambridge, MA: Cambridge University Press.

Menn, Lise and Nina F. Dronkers. 2016. *Psycholinguistics: Introduction and Applications*, second edition. San Diego: Plural Publishing.

Merriam-Webster. 1961. *Webster's Third New International Dictionary of the English Language, Unabridged*. Springfield, MA: Merriam-Webster.

Merriam-Webster. 2003. *Merriam-Webster's Collegiate Dictionary*, eleventh edition. Springfield, MA: Merriam-Webster.

Mifsud, Rob. 2012. "How Americans near the Great Lakes Are Radically Changing the Sound of English." *Slate*. www.slate.com/articles/life/the_good_word/2012/08/northern_cities_vowel_shift_how_americans_in_the_great_lakes_region_are_revolutionizing_english_.html

Millar, Robert McColl, editor. 2015. *Trask's Historical Linguistics*, third edition. Abingdon/New York: Routledge.

Mitkov, Ruslan, editor. 2005. *The Oxford Handbook of Computational Linguistics*. Oxford: Oxford University Press.

Miura, Shion (Juliet Winters Carpenter, translator). 2017. *The Great Passage*. Seattle: Amazon Crossing. Originally published 2011 as *Fune o amu*. Tokyo: Kobunsha Co., Ltd.

"Multiple Modals." *Yale Grammatical Diversity Project*. https://ygdp.yale.edu/phenomena/multiple-modals

Murphy, Lynne. 2018. *The Prodigal Tongue: The Love-Hate Relationship between American and British English*. New York: Penguin USA.

Murphy, Lynne. *Separated by a Common Language* (blog). https://separatedbyacommonlanguage.blogspot.com

Nagle, Traci. 2013. Review of *Hobson-Jobson: The Definitive Glossary of British India by Henry Yule and A.C. Burnell*, selected edition, edited by Kate Teltscher. *Dictionaries: Journal of the Dictionary Society of North America*. Volume 34, number 1, pages 225–229.

Nettle, Daniel and Suzanne Romaine. 2002. *Vanishing Voices: The Extinction of the World's Languages*. New York/Oxford: Oxford University Press.

Nurse, Derek and Gérard Philippson, editors. 2003. *The Bantu Languages*. Abingdon/New York: Routledge.

Okrent, Arika. 2016. "11 Fun Facts about the International Phonetic Alphabet." *Mental Floss* (blog). http://mentalfloss.com/article/83340/11-fun-facts-about-international-phonetic-alphabet

Orton, Harold, Stewart Sanderson, and John Widdowson, editors. 1978. *The Linguistic Atlas of England*. London: Croom Helm Ltd. (Reprinted 1996 London: Routledge).

Ottenheimer, Harriet Joseph. 2013. *The Anthropology of Language: An Introduction to Linguistic Anthropology*, third edition. Belmont, CA: Wadsworth, Cengage Learning.

Our Dialects: Mapping Variation in English in the UK. The University of Manchester. http://projects.alc.manchester.ac.uk/ukdialectmaps

Oxford English Dictionary. 2011. *Oxford English Dictionary*, third edition. Oxford: Oxford University Press.

Oxford English Dictionary. 2014. "Alleyways of Language: Regional Words for 'Alleyway'." *Oxford Dictionaries* (blog). https://blog.oxforddictionaries.com/2014/10/regional-words-alleyway/

Pépiot, Erwan. 2013. "Voice, Speech and Gender: Male-Female Acoustic Differences and Cross-Language Variation in English and French Speakers." *XVèmes Rencontres Jeunes Chercheurs de l'ED 268, June 2012 Paris, France. (à paraître)*. <halshs-00764811> https://halshs.archives-ouvertes.fr/halshs-00764811

Perlman, Merrill. 2016. "Will 'They' Ever Change?" *Columbia Journalism Review* (Language Corner blog). April 11, 2016. https://cjr.org/language_corner/will_they_ever_change.php

Pinker, Steven. 1994. *The Language Instinct*. New York: W. W. Morrow.

Pinker, Steven. 2014. *The Sense of Style*. New York: Viking.

Poplack, Shana and Sali Tagliamonte. 2001. *African American English in the Diaspora*. Malden/Oxford: Wiley-Blackwell.

Pullum, Geoffrey K. 1999. "African American Vernacular English Is Not Standard English with Mistakes." In *The Workings of Language*, edited by Rebecca S. Wheeler. Pages 39–58. Westport, CT: Prager.

Pullum, Geoffrey K. and William A. Ladusaw. 1996. *Phonetic Style Guide*, second edition. Chicago: University of Chicago Press.

Rickford, John R. 2015. "The Creole Origins Hypothesis." In *The Oxford Handbook of African American Language*, edited by Sonja Lanehart. Pages 35–56. Oxford/New York: Oxford University Press.

Rickford, John R. and Russell J. Rickford. 2000. *Spoken Soul: The Story of Black English*. New York: Wiley.

Rowland, Caroline. 2014. *Understanding Child Language Acquisition*. Abingdon/New York: Routledge.

Saussure, Ferdinand de. 1916. *Course in General Linguistics (Cours de linguistique générale)*, edited by Charles Bally and Albert Sechehaye with the collaboration of Albert Riedlinger. Paris: Editions Payot. 1983 translation of 1972 Editions Payot (Paris) version by Roy Harris, and published (1986), LaSalle, IL: Open Court Publishing Company.

Schieffelin, Bambi, Kathryn A. Woolard, and Paul V. Kroskrity, editors. 1998. *Language Ideologies: Practice and Theory*. New York/Oxford: Oxford University Press.

Schiffrin, Deborah, Deborah Tannen, and Heidi E. Hamilton, editors. 2001. *The Handbook of Discourse Analysis*. Malden/Oxford: Blackwell Publishers.

Searle, John. 1989. "How Performatives Work." *Linguistics and Philosophy*. Volume 12, pages 535–558. (Reprinted in Susumu Kubo and Daniel Vanderveken, editors. 2002. *Essays in Speech Act Theory*. Amsterdam: John Benjamins Publishing Company).

Sebba, Mark. 1997. *Contact Languages: Pidgins and Creoles*. Basingstoke/London: Macmillan Press and New York: St. Martin's Press.

Shakespeare, William. c. 1595. *Romeo & Juliet*. http://shakespeare.mit.edu/romeo_juliet/full.html

Shakespeare, Willam. c. 1599. *Hamlet*. http://shakespeare.mit.edu/hamlet/full.html

Shakespeare, William. 1602. *Troilus & Cressida*. http://shakespeare.mit.edu/troilus_cressida/full.html

Shakespeare, William. 2004. *Romeo & Juliet*, Folger Shakespeare Library edition. New York: Simon & Schuster.

Shakespeare, William. 2007. *Troilus & Cressida*, Folger Shakespeare Library edition. New York: Simon & Schuster.

Shakespeare, William. 2012. *Hamlet*, Folger Shakespeare Library edition. New York: Simon & Schuster.

Sheidlower, Jesse. 2017. "The Closing of a Great American Dialect Project." *The New Yorker* (blog). September 22, 2017. https://newyorker.com/culture/cultural-comment/the-closing-of-a-great-american-dialect-project

Skinner, David. 2012–2013. *The Story of Ain't*. New York: Harper Perennial.

Sperber, Dan and Deirdre Wilson. 1995. *Relevance: Communication and Cognition*, second edition. Malden/Oxford: Blackwell Publishers.

Stamper, Kory. 2017. *Word by Word*. New York: Pantheon Books.

Stamper, Kory. *Harmless Drudgery* (blog). https://korystamper.wordpress.com

Stevens, Kenneth N. 2000. *Acoustic Phonetics*. Cambridge: MIT University Press.

Strunk, William, Jr. and E. B. White. 1959. *The Elements of Style*. New York: Macmillan.

Tallerman, Maggie. 2014. *Understanding Syntax*, fourth edition. Abingdon/New York: Routledge.

Tannen, Deborah. 1994. *Gender and Discourse*. New York: Oxford University Press.

Tannen, Deborah. 2005. *Conversational Style: Analyzing Talk among Friends*, revised edition. Oxford/New York: Oxford University Press.

Thomason, Sarah. 2001. *Language Contact: An Introduction*. Edinburgh: Edinburgh University Press.

Tocharian and Indo-European Studies. Copenhagen: The Museum Tusculanum Press.

Traxler, Matthew J. 2011. *Introduction to Psycholinguistics*. Malden/Oxford/Chichester: Wiley-Blackwell.

Truss, Lynne. 2004. *Eats, Shoots & Leaves: The Zero Tolerance Approach to Punctuation*. New York: Gotham Books.

University of Chicago Press. *Chicago Manual of Style*, seventeenth edition. 2017. Chicago: University of Chicago Press.

van Bezooijen, Reneé. 1995. "Sociocultural Aspects of Pitch Differences between Japanese and Dutch Women." *Language and Speech*. Volume 38, number 3, pages 253–265.

Vaux, Bert and Scott Golder. 2003. *The Harvard Dialect Survey*. Cambridge, MA: Harvard University Linguistics Department.

Velupillai, Viveka. 2012. *An Introduction to Linguistic Typology*. Amsterdam/Philadelphia: John Benjamins Publishing Company.

Vendler, Zeno. 1957. "Verbs and Times." *The Philosophical Review*. Volume 66, number 2, pages 143–160.

Watkins, Calvert, editor. 2011. *The American Heritage Dictionary of Indo-European Roots*, third edition. Boston: Houghton Mifflin Harcourt.

Watterson, Bill. 1993. "Calvin and Hobbes." *Verbing Weirds Language* panel. January 25, 1993. www.gocomics.com/calvinandhobbes/1993/01/25

Webster's New World Dictionaries. 2018. *Webster's New World College Dictionary*, fifth edition. Boston/New York: Houghton Mifflin Harcourt.

Whynot, Lauri A. 2017. *Understanding International Sign: A Sociolinguistic Study*, Sociolinguistics in Deaf Communities, volume 22. Washington: Gallaudet University Press.

Williams, Ann and Paul Kerswill. 1999. "Dialect Levelling: Change and Continuity in Milton Keynes, Reading and Hull." In *Urban Voices: Accent Studies in the British Isles*, edited by Paul Foulkes and Gerard Docherty. Pages 141–162. London: Arnold.

Winchester, Simon. 1998. *The Professor and the Madman*. New York City: Harper Perennial.

Winer, Lise, editor. 2009. *Dictionary of the English/Creole of Trinidad & Tobago*. Montreal: McGill – Queen's University Press.

Winford, Donald. 2003. *An Introduction to Contact Linguistics*. Malden/Oxford/Chichester: Wiley-Blackwell.

Wolf, Naomi. 2015. "Young Women, Give Up the Vocal Fry and Reclaim Your Strong Female Voice." *The Guardian*. July 24, 2015. https://theguardian.com/commentisfree/2015/jul/24/vocal-fry-strong-female-voice

Wolfram, Walt and Erik R. Thomas. 2002. *The Development of African American English*. Malden/Oxford/Chichester: Wiley-Blackwell.

Wolfram, Walt and Ben Ward, editors. 2008. *American Voices*. Malden/Oxford/Chichester: Wiley-Blackwell.

Yin, Karen. *Conscious Style Guide* (blog). http://consciousstyleguide.com

Societies, associations, and university projects

ACES: The Society for Editing: aceseditors.org

American Association of Applied Linguistics: aaal.org

American Dialect Society: americandialect.org

British Association for Applied Linguistics: baal.org.uk

Canadian Association of Applied Linguistics: aclacaal.org

Canadian Linguistic Association: cla-acl.ca

Dialect Atlas of Newfoundland and Labrador: dialectatlas.mun.ca

Dictionary Society of North America: dictionarysociety.com

Endangered Language Project: endangeredlanguages.com

Euralex: euralex.org

International Phonetic Association: internationalphoneticassociation.org

Linguistic Society of America: linguisticsociety.org

Linguistics Association for Great Britain: lagb.org.uk

Our Dialects (University of Manchester): projects.alc.manchester.ac.uk/
ukdialectmaps

Purdue Online Writing Lab: owl.english.purdue.edu/owl/

Society for Pidgin and Creole Linguistics: sites.google.com/site/society
pidgncreolelinguistics

Yale Grammatical Diversity Project: ygdp.yale.edu

Yorkshire Dialect Society: yorkshiredialectsociety.org.uk

Index